HOW TO FORECAST
A Guide for Business

To my wife, Margaret
for her unwavering support

To the memory of James Morrell who started forecasting in
1955 and until his death in September 2000 dedicated his life
to giving advice and assistance in business forecasting to help
small and intermediate companies, who were unlikely to have
a team of forecasters, or alternatively to give an independent
view of company plans and to look ahead at least five and
possibly as far as fifteen years ahead. In fact, his forecasts
were taken by blue chip companies as well as smaller firms.
He was always available to give advice by seminars or in-
house consultations and assistance in forecasting matters,
specializing in the Housing Market and Motor trades until his
retirement in April 2000.

James Morrell waited until his retirement in April 2000 to
write this book. His aim was to assist CEOs, Marketing
Directors, Planners and Analysts to look ahead for at least
five years; for planning budgets and marketing, bringing
attention to the fact that nothing is decided without a
forecast. He used no jargon, preferred short sentences with
bold diagrams to give a clear message. So far as business is
concerned he felt it essential to set out various scenarios and
put odds on the possibilities in order to make the firm more
flexible, more positive in its operations and with the final
objective of greater efficiency, job satisfaction and ultimately
better returns.

Margaret Morrell

HOW TO FORECAST

A guide for business

James Morrell

Gower

Published by
Gower Publishing Limited
Gower House
Croft Road
Aldershot
Hampshire GU11 3HR
England

Gower Publishing Company
131 Main Street
Burlington VT 05401–5600 USA

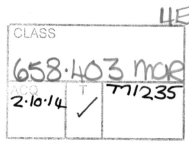

British Library Cataloguing in Publication Data
Morrell, James
   How to forecast : a guide for business
   1. Business forecasting
   I. Title
   658.4'0355
ISBN 0 566 08363 9
ISBN 0 566 08492 9

Library of Congress Cataloging-in-Publication Data
Morrell, James
      How to forecast : a guide for business / James Morrell.
         p. cm.
      Includes bibliographical references.
      ISBN 0-566-08363-9 (hardcover)
      ISBN 0-566-08492-9 (paperback)
      1. Business forecasting. I. Title

   HD30.27 .M67 2001
   658.4'035–dc21   2001033392

Typeset in Plantin Light by IML Typographers, Birkenhead and printed in Great Britain by TJ International Ltd., Padstow, Cornwall.

CONTENTS

LIST OF DIAGRAMS

LIST OF TABLES

FOREWORD

James Morrell was more than the father figure of business forecasting. As this book makes abundantly and powerfully clear, he remained among its most convincing practitioners. Published posthumously, this fascinating work brings to life the special qualities which set Jimmy apart. He saw with total clarity that the future can only be read through deep understanding of the present, and that the present can only be understood on a foundation of thorough knowledge of the past.

His own combination of erudition and intuition is displayed on every one of these pages. He was a hard-headed witness of human frailty, and no Panglossian. To Jimmy, things were definitely not for the best in the best of all possible worlds: he never denied realities, pleasant or unpleasant, vile or good. One good outweighed much evil, however; taking the long view of human history, the conditions of human life, despite upheavals and horrors caused by nature and man, have improved wonderfully overall. This book carefully examines the reasons why this extraordinary advance might stop – and concludes that, on the whole, it is likely to continue.

It would be foolish – and foolhardy – to argue against this closely reasoned conclusion. But Jimmy's careful observation of past and present led him, rightly, to be sceptical about mankind's ability to manage the planet and its innumerable sub-divisions. Coping with natural hazards alone presents enough challenges, but 'with few exceptions the risks confronting mankind are of its own creation'. Not only has mankind created the problems of population growth, industrialization and the polluted environment, but its leaders have been singularly inept at dealing with these self-made threats.

As Jimmy argued, without an improvement in governmental capability and performance, the risks from these failures must become intolerable. Even where governments have been relatively successful – notably, since 1945, in sustaining historically high economic growth – they have wrestled unsuccessfully with the consequences. Here, the issue which especially concerns him is the potentially cancerous shortage of jobs, as technology reduces the demand for an increasing supply of labour. He was by no means sure that effective answers to unemployment would be found; and that reinforced his other reasons for expecting a slowdown in world economic growth as the 21st century progressed.

Recession cannot be ruled out, on this sobering analysis. But if 'the leading economic powers' (which will include a China easily outstripping the USA) 'fail to collaborate effectively to counter those trends, recession could develop into long-drawn-out depression, with further serious social and political consequences'. This warning element in the book makes Jimmy sound like a doom-sayer, but that is far from the truth. His essential, though qualified, optimism shines through its pages and their contemplation of man's insatiable progress, of the 'virtually limitless' expansion of human knowledge and of humanity's equally limitless opportunities.

That emphasis on human powers and their potentially benevolent unfolding (for major instance, in lesser risk of international conflict and war) marks James Morrell as a radical humanist, as a worthy heir to the rich tradition of true British liberal values. Very high among those values is dispassionate fact-based analysis by thinkers who personally lack neither passion nor principle. Long years ago, these qualities drew me to Jimmy, as the ideal economic forecaster for a magazine (*Management Today*) which needed to discover what was really happening in business in order to help management achieve improved outcomes.

Like so many others who read his writings, heard his excellent addresses or benefited from his counsel, I only came to admire him more and more, as a professional and as a friend. Sad as we are to lose him, we can take some consolation in a far-ranging but penetrating book that serves admirably as James Morrell's own, inspiring epitaph.

Robert Heller, Management Author

INTRODUCTION: THE ROLE OF FORECASTING

Every decision rests on a forecast – a view of the future. We know from everyday experience that many of the forecasts we are obliged to make will prove mistaken. Yet this does not invalidate the case for basing decisions upon forecasts. We are obliged to formulate forecasts of some kind or other as a means of determining a future course of action.

Man has evolved into a highly successful surviving animal. His chances of success have been enhanced by his ability to foresee the consequences of his decisions. In that sense we are all forecasters.

Forecasting is an essential discipline in planning and running a business. Success depends, to a large extent, on getting those forecasts right. We know, however, that the future is highly uncertain. Throughout our lives we are confronted with uncertainties. There is, therefore, a fair chance that we will not make the right decisions.

In business we are continually confronted by the need to take decisions. The important decisions compel us to construct a route map of the future and to forecast which way our decisions will take us. A wrong decision can end in disaster. For that reason we need to bring a wide range of skills to bear on the possible and probable outcomes of the decisions.

The business environment is constantly changing. It has become increasingly complex. Large organizations have the capacity to set up specialist units to provide forecasts for a wide range of subjects. All firms need to forecast the level of sales and revenues. This may require commissioned market research to establish the pattern of the market, its size and its growth potential.

The firm will also require an analysis of the competition, an appraisal of product design and development and an assessment of pricing policy. This also leads to an analysis of costs, covering labour and purchase of materials, components and services. The cost of capital may also be relevant, as will premises and location.

The network of related items needed for a thorough analysis and a set of forecasts relating to sales will include a number of crucial areas where we have no control. We cannot control interest rates, exchange rates, commodity prices, taxation and legislation. We cannot control the labour market or the levels and changes in the customers' spending power. Yet it is just as important to forecast those factors which are beyond our control as to forecast those which we can control.

All businesses will be affected by changes in taxation and interest rates. No business can escape the rises and falls of the business cycle. It is therefore essential to have an understanding of the causes of cyclical fluctuations and to make allowances for those potential fluctuations in building up a set of forecasts.

The object of forecasting

This may be summarized as: 'to minimize uncertainty and to identify and evaluate risk'. Faced with doubts about the future the decision-taker requires as much information about the past and the future as is possible. He will need to know how much risk attaches to alternative decisions.

For these reasons, the problem of forecasting needs to be approached in as scientific a manner as possible. Yet it is as well at the outset to keep in mind the imprecise nature of many of the subjects to be forecast. Not only is our knowledge of the future extremely limited but our knowledge of the past is far from complete. There are few truly dependable sets of statistics describing the past and the margin of error in many of the series in common use is wide – in some cases so wide as to invalidate statistical analysis.

Thus forecasting must continue to be regarded very much as an art rather than a science, in spite of the continuous advances in computer technology. A golden rule of the computer industry is 'rubbish in equals rubbish out'. Subjective judgement will be called into play at many points in the construction of a set of forecasts and the forecaster's judgement will be more dependable if he has a strong grounding in history and a feel for the passage of time and the pace of change. He has to be armed with a storehouse of knowledge about the subject in question, to know the sources of the relevant statistics and – above all – to know how dependable (or unreliable) these sources may be.

It is in this respect that forecasting is an art rather than a science and the greater the forecaster's experience the better. This does not mean that scientific methods should not be employed. The statistical techniques for calculating a trend or a relationship are obviously scientific.

The range of forecasts

A wide range of business management problems involve forecasting. Forecasts are required not only for the annual budget and the business plan but for the appraisal of investment projects, the commissioning and exploitation of research as well as the appraisal of competition and the feasibility of making acquisitions. Thus a large part of management activity – the critical part of management – calls for research and forecasting work of one kind or another.

Throughout life each man is his own forecaster. So it tends to be in business. Yet the instances where it will be necessary to set down the forecasts in a systematic fashion have increased. This is not to say that detailed forecasts have to be supplied for every decision and every problem. Forecasting is an exacting task which will absorb a substantial amount of management time. Sophisticated forecasts must be constructed only where the forecasts make a direct contribution towards the problem in hand. There should be a return on the effort and cost of a piece of forecasting as with any other investment in managerial time. Sledgehammers must not be used to crack nuts.

Equally, a common body of forecasting will serve a number of purposes within the firm. The large corporation comprising a number of subsidiaries and/or separate divisions may well find that each unit needs to forecast some similar, common subjects. In these cases forecasting may be regarded as a function conducted for the business as a whole. A set of forecasts in which the parts are consistent with the sum should be agreed centrally and made available for the various parts of the firm. Ideally, therefore, forecasting effort should be directed centrally and come under the control of the chief executive's office.

Yet there are discordant views about forecasting. Warren Buffet, the hugely successful American long-term investor, said in his annual report of March 1995, 'We will continue to ignore political and economic forecasts, which are an expensive distraction for many investors and businessmen.' I have met a number of company chairmen over the years who have bluntly said they did not believe in forecasting. These were generally autocrats surrounded by yes men. In committee the boss pronounced his judgements and the discussion proceeded to rubber-stamp them.

Now this is plain stupid. We all know that there are many uncertainties lying in wait for us. But the art of living and surviving successfully is to attempt to foresee the pitfalls surrounding the opportunities that lie ahead and to work out the likely outcome of our decisions. The unforeseen events – not all adverse by the way – present the major risks which have to be assessed in weighing up the odds on our forecasts being fulfilled and the costs of things turning out badly. Mr Buffet is very hot on making sufficient risk allowances.

This is a vital aspect of forecasting which is seldom given proper attention. Through my career the demand has generally been for a single 'best bet' set of forecasts: perfectly understandable since most executives' lives are taken up with day-to-day administration, leaving little time to keep informed about the changes unfolding in the great big outside world and almost no time for educative reading and (even more importantly) constructive thinking.

Organizing the data and the forecasts

Most firms have a deeply entrenched calendar with timetables embracing all departments for submission of annual budgets and similar timetables for drawing up plans for two years ahead or longer. These are often regarded down the line as chores imposed on an already overloaded timetable. Plans, where they are made, are often extensions of the budget.

Forecasting has become more difficult because of the acceleration in technological change and the speeding up of communications. This has not been matched by any improvement in the collection of economic and social statistics. The margins for error are just as big and anyone who has been involved in the compilation of returns to government departments or business surveys will be aware of the sources of inaccuracies.

My object in writing this book is to draw on the experience of a long working lifetime to provide guidance in forecasting over the range of topics with which businesses are concerned and to help the busy executive to deal with the uncertainties and the problems raised by unreliable data. For that purpose I have divided the subject matter between those subjects over which the business has no control from those where it has virtually complete control.

Diagram I.1 shows the main factors of the environment in which the business has to operate and for which it may have to construct forecasts. Those outside the firm's direct control are extremely powerful and affect all businesses to a greater or lesser degree.

Climate

Variations in climate may affect crops and harvests and may generate shortages or surpluses which will lead to major movements in food prices. Equally, abnormal changes in temperature will change demand, as with hot spells raising the demand for cold drinks and ice cream, or an unusual cold spell depressing sales of cold items and raising demand for hot food and drink.

In a wider scenario, natural disasters arising from volcanic activity and earthquakes can disrupt the economies of large areas and the climatic effects of El Niño, which occurs with varying intensity at intervals of around five years, are quite dramatic. The warming of the eastern Pacific which generates El Niño results in excessive rainfall in some regions and destructive droughts in others, spanning huge areas of the world.

Diagram I.1   The business environment

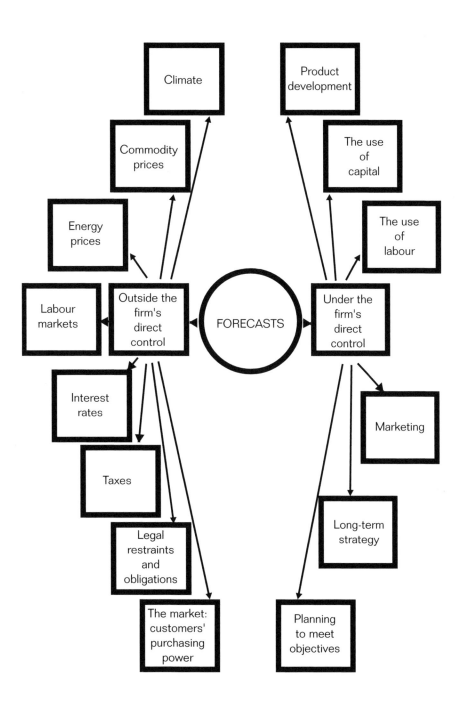

Climatic variations are minor factors for the great majority of businesses. An important minority, however, has to be prepared to face the consequences of fluctuations in weather and climate which may make a major impact on the price of supplies and demand for the firm's products.

Commodity prices

Apart from food crops, rubber, wool and cotton are raw materials which are subject to major swings in prices. These may be affected by climate. They are also subject to substantial changes in demand resulting from the swings in the world business cycle. Above-average rises in spending and output in the world's major economies will tend to force up the prices of raw materials in the commodity markets. Conversely, a downturn in the world business cycle will depress demand and prices in the industrial commodity markets. Metal prices, including precious metals, are equally subject to large swings, and firms depending on commodity supplies will need to forecast change in prices as part of their budgeting and marketing exercises.

Energy prices

Energy accounts for a large part of costs in the manufacturing industry. Metal manufacture uses vast amounts of energy, whilst electricity production is the dominant customer for raw energy. Transport, too, has large energy costs. Approximately 10 per cent of national costs arise from energy demand, the majority arising from industrial production. Energy costs are a minor item for the majority of service activities.

Labour markets

Labour accounts for over half of total costs in most national economies. Very large numbers of people change jobs during the course of a year and the labour market determines the level of wages and salaries. Governments and trade unions have considerable influence on the labour market but the fact remains that supply and demand determine the levels of pay in regional markets and industries.

Most firms operate in urban areas where there are many other businesses and the going rates of pay in those areas are determined by the labour market. Where pay levels are low the firm will run the risk of losing labour to its competitors. In that sense the labour market is beyond the individual firm's direct control and its policy with regard to pay and conditions of service will be strongly influenced by the wide labour market in which it operates.

Interest rates and exchange rates

Most firms borrow and pay interest. In many cases stocks and work-in-progress are financed by bank loans on which the bank charges a variable rate of interest. Firms may also borrow to help finance expansion and long-term investment in the business is financed in part by the issue of bonds.

Changes in interest rates may have a profound effect on a firm. Should rates be raised with the object of dampening down the demand for credit and the growth in spending, the check to spending will reduce sales for some sectors and damage profits. There is thus an indirect impact on a firm's fortunes as well as a direct effect insofar as the firm has to pay a higher rate of interest on its borrowings.

The rate of interest is fixed by the central bank and is outside the firm's control. Thus this powerful factor affecting business prospects can have a major impact on the firm in both directions, stimulating business via lower interest rates and retarding it via higher rates. Prudent management obliges the firm to anticipate the likelihood of changes in interest rates and to forecast the consequences.

Interest rates also have a bearing on exchange rates. Exchange rate movements are reflected in both export and import prices and this is another important area of business over which the firm has no control.

Taxation

Similarly, the levels of taxation are beyond the firm's control. In some cases governments signal changes in taxation in advance, but this is not the general rule. The firm must therefore assess to what extent its sales may be affected by changes in sales tax or value added tax or excise duties and whether changes in corporation tax and allowances may distort its cash flow.

Legal restraints

Part of the business environment is dictated by laws and regulations. Health and safety legislation will determine certain standards that businesses must maintain. Equally, employment contracts may be regulated by legislation and in many countries free competition is maintained by legal restraints against monopolies. All these matters are beyond the control of the individual firm.

Customers' spending power

Finally, the firm cannot control its own markets. It may endeavour to do so by differentiating its products from other competing brands but in broad terms it cannot determine how much money its potential customers have to spend. Government policy will influence spending power through changes in both taxation and interest rates and a country's export markets will be heavily influenced by the changes in spending power in other countries. None of these features can be controlled by the individual firm.

Yet there is a clutch of activities over which the firm has complete control and which we now consider.

Product development

The firm will obviously decide the products and services which it will make. Its decisions will be influenced by its forecasts of markets and their potential. Unless restrained by patents it will be free to design what it plans to make and sell.

The use of capital

A business has complete control of its capital and is able to decide the extent to which it borrows and timing and scale of new stock market issues. It is obviously subject to the regulations with regard to share and bond issues and the scope of its borrowing will be limited by considerations of risk on the part of the lenders.

The use of labour

Although pay rates are dictated by the local labour market, the firm is not inhibited in the management of its workforce except insofar as regulations lay down the boundaries for working hours and holidays and such items as a minimum wage. The firm can plan recruitment and the training of its staff and make provision for pensions.

In forecasting its manpower requirements it will be necessary to take account of those features of the business environment which will influence the growth of the firm and timing of change.

Marketing

The business has complete control of its marketing and is able to promote its products so as to optimize its sales revenue, taking into account the changes in the level of the market in response to changes in the economic environment.

Long-term strategy and objectives

In planning long-term strategy it is necessary to take into account all aspects of the business environment likely to bear on the firm's activities. Although strategic planning is an activity entirely within the firm's control it is nevertheless concerned with those factors outside its control. Planning must not be carried out in a vacuum. It must make allowances for the timing and pattern of change and for the action of competitors.

Ideally, the firm should agree its objectives. These are likely to include product development, growth in sales, profit margins and return on capital. Having set the objectives the plan should outline the ways and means of reaching those targets. This will include the use of manpower, the generation of capital, investment to maintain and increase capacity and efficiency, the provision of premises and the profile of costs.

In all these aspects of management, forecasting has a role to play and the following chapters outline the approach and forecasting routines for the various subjects of concern to the business.

PART *1*

BEYOND THE FIRM'S CONTROL

1 FORECASTING THE NATIONAL ECONOMY

Most business forecasts are derived from a forecast of the national economy. A forecast of a particular domestic market or an industry, has to take account of the changes in national spending power and output. This does not mean that the firm has to construct a detailed forecast of the national economy.

There are large numbers of forecasts made by banks, stockbrokers and forecasting institutions and it is possible to use one of these to provide a background forecast for the firm's specific needs. It is essential, however, for the firm's forecaster to check the assumptions used in the national forecast. It is not difficult to vary some of the assumptions and to modify the statistical picture of the whole economy.

Consensus forecasts are also available, built up from a large number of national forecasts. These, however, must be treated with caution since there are no consensus assumptions and it is not possible to amend the consensus figures for a variation in assumptions. The consensus forecast may show high and low figures for the various components of the forecast and these may give some clue as to the degree of certainty and uncertainty of the different features.

In order to understand forecasting techniques it is necessary to analyse the construction of the national income accounts and how the economy works.

The measurement of national product

The product of the economy can be measured in three ways: first, by summing all the incomes of the community; second, by summing all the spending of the community; and third, by summing the value of the output. By definition the three measures of product must be equal. This is because all income is either spent or saved; and savings are also spent in one way or another by the body which uses the savings. Thus the total of spending on both goods and services for current consumption, and on capital investment in fixed assets and stocks, must be equal to total income.

Similarly, output gives rise to income, in the form either of wages and salaries or of profits. Profits are as much a form of income as wages and salaries and are either distributed in the form of interest and dividends or else retained as business savings. The fact remains, however, that output has a revenue value which is equal to the income it generates. Therefore output must also equal incomes. Thus, for purposes of measurement and estimation of the national product and national income, incomes = spending = output.

This sequence is illustrated in Diagram 1.1. It will be seen that at each point of time income, spending and output are equal. It will also be seen that income leads to spending and spending generates output. The diagram also illustrates the role of stocks, since spending will first affect the level of stocks held in the retailers' hands. Changes at the retail level will result in new orders directly, or through wholesalers, to factories and this in turn will generate orders for new production.

Diagram 1.1 National product flows

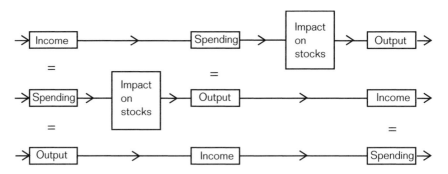

Diagram 1.2 National product growth spiral

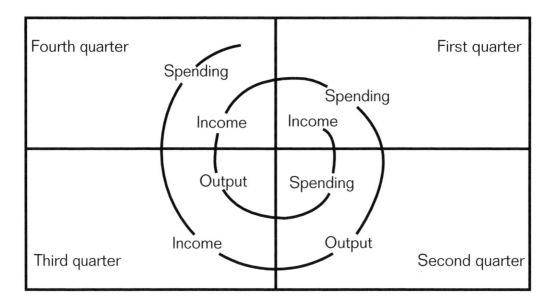

The sequence is further illustrated in Diagram 1.2, using the simple assumption that there are time lags of roughly three months between changes in income and changes in spending and then intervals of three months between changes in spending and changes in output. It will be seen that the sequence can be thought of as a spiral. In a growing economy, the cycle of cause and effect, moving through income to spending to output, will result in income in the second round being higher than in the first round. Although it is difficult to illustrate the process diagrammatically, the chart of the spiral could be enlarged to show three simultaneous spirals with the income spending and output factors being equal at each point in time.

The first stage in forecasting, therefore, has to be the construction of a consistent set of estimates of data for the past. This is a problem which has received far too little analytical attention in all countries. It is regrettable to find that considerable research resources are devoted to exploring relationships between the economic sectors instead of giving priority to the improvement of the statistical raw material. Analysts tend to be dazzled by figures and frequently overlook the poor quality of the statistics they manipulate. In many cases fine research is unjustified because of the crudeness of the available data.

The National Income Accounts show estimates of the broad measures of product broken down into considerable detail. The forecaster then has to marshal the statistics in such a way as to draw out the sequence of cause and effect and to trace changes throughout the whole system.

Money flows

The simple concept of incomes generating spending and then production via an impact on stocks must also be seen in relation to the stock and flow of money.

Organizations and individuals hold money in the form of both bank accounts and cash, bank deposits being by far and away the more important. Spending decisions depend not only on the receipt of income but also on cash in hand and at bank and expectations of income in the future. A convenient way to think about income and spending is that incomes 'top up' the individual's (or organization's) stock of cash before it is depleted by spending.

A simplified illustration of the concept of stock and flows of money is shown in Diagram 1.3. Moving from output (bottom left) through to incomes in the form of wages and profits, tax is then paid over to the government. What is left is 'disposable' income, available for spending.

In fact the incomes after tax are added to the money stock and individuals (and businesses) spend out of their replenished money stock. Part of the

Diagram 1.3 Government and the economy

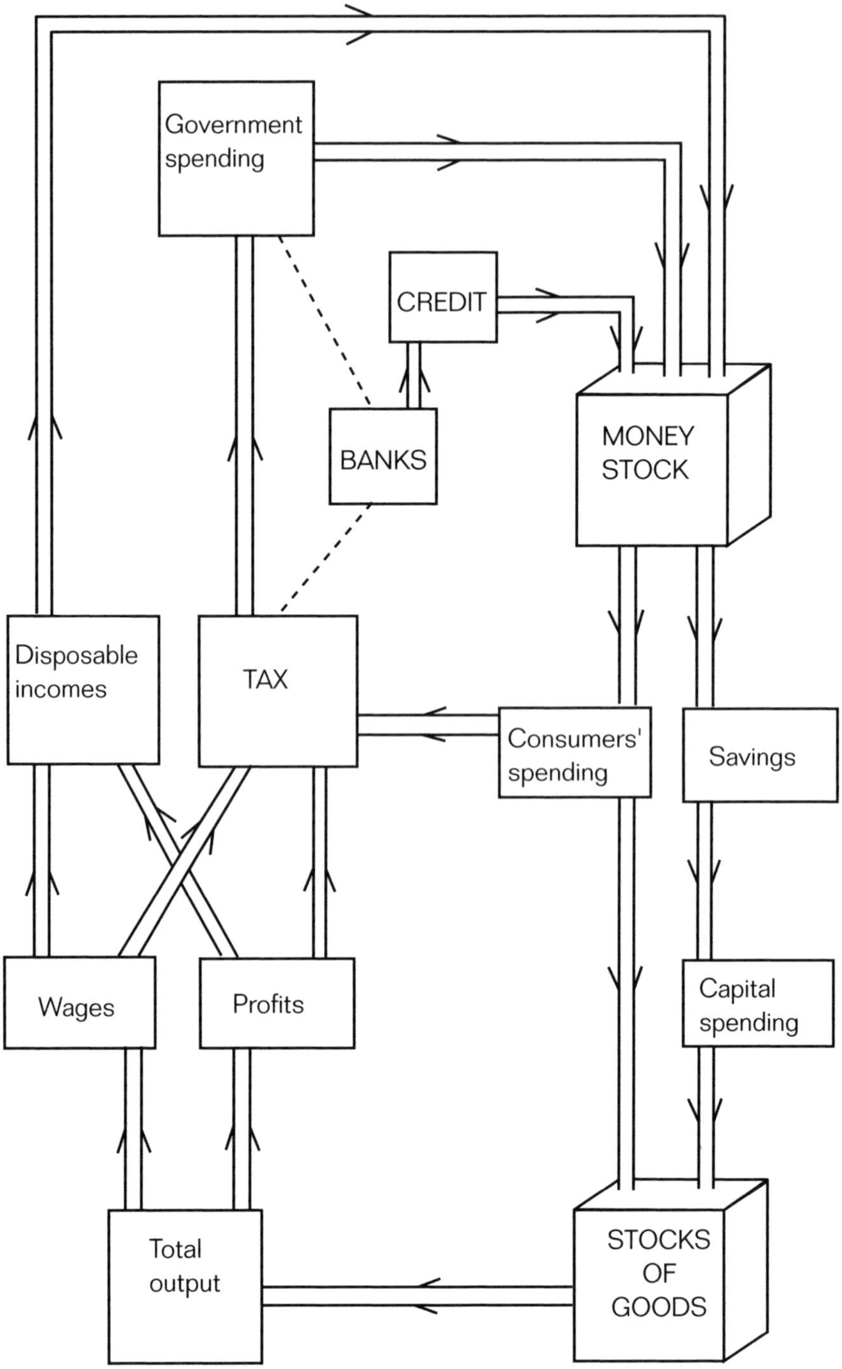

disposable incomes will be saved and in the first instance the savings swell the money stocks. In practice, businesses and individuals spend not only on consumer goods but also on capital goods, and the money stock will be depleted by capital spending.

Spending then makes its impact on the stock of goods, before making an impact via orders for new production. Total output includes capital goods as well as consumer products and services. Spending on services, of course, is not 'intercepted' by stocks. A haircut is performed on the spot.

Thus the money goes round and round and economic life proceeds in an unchanging way. How, then, do things change? There are five main factors to take into account, namely, government policy and its impact on incomes and spending; government financing and its impact on the banking system; monetary policy; imports and exports and transactions with the outside world; and finally, technical changes, altering the way things are produced and the way people live.

Government fiscal policy

Government takes money away from the public by way of taxation. The money is put back via government spending. Increases in taxation and decreases in government spending reduce the public's spending power; the opposite policy changes increase spending power. In practice, governments (like businesses) nearly always run a surplus on current account; that is, government revenues exceed public authorities' current account spending on goods and services, the principal items being education, defence and health.

The surplus on current account is nearly always insufficient to finance public sector capital spending. The deficits have to be financed by borrowing. In practice, an increase in the deficit means more money is being added to the private sector's bank balance and a decrease results in a smaller addition to private bank balances and spending capacity

Monetary policy

Public sector deficits are financed by two forms of borrowing: by tapping private savings by selling government bonds and by borrowing from the banking system via the issue of Treasury Bills (three-month IOUs).

When the financial institutions and other private bodies buy bonds they in effect hand back to the government part of the money pushed out as a result of the public sector overall deficit. When the banks lend the government money via purchases of Treasury Bills their ability to lend is not diminished because Treasury Bills rank as near cash in banks' balance sheets. Thus, whereas the government gets the use of the money it has borrowed via Treasury Bills, the banks' (and general public's) cash resources are undiminished.

Part of the shortfall is also met by issuing new notes and coin, but increases in cash in circulation generally contribute a minor part in financing an increase in the money supply.

One of the basic rules of banking is that 'every advance creates its own deposit'. This is because an overdraft facility leads the borrower to draw cheques which make their way into other bank accounts. Other banks' deposit levels therefore rise and the banks are in turn able to lend more. The net result is a rise in deposits overall, tending to match the initial increase in bank advances. Thus an increase in the money supply, resulting from government deficit financing, will tend to be increased still further by extra bank lending, providing the banks are willing to lend and the general public willing to borrow.

Expansion of credit can, of course, be controlled or neutralized by the authorities. Special deposits or forced loans from the banks can be employed to 'mop up' surplus funds from the banks. In addition, direct controls can be applied to bank lending, either rationing credit or creating special classes of borrowers.

The authorities can also borrow abroad, or foreigners may bring extra funds into (or take funds out of) the country, thus influencing the money supply (discussed below).

Interest rates are the 'price' of money. Extra money in relation to the demand for funds will tend to reduce interest rates and vice versa. If the authorities wish to manipulate interest rates it is necessary to allow the money supply to change in relation to the demand for funds. Thus, if interest rates are fixed, money supply will need to fluctuate; if money supply is fixed then interest rates will need to fluctuate.

The outside world

Imports and exports of goods and services seldom balance out. The net of these items is usually the biggest feature in the balance of payments. Other current payments, in and out, of such things as interest, dividends, foreign aid and emigrants' remittances, together with the trade balance, make up the balance of payments on current account.

Capital movements comprising business investment in both directions, portfolio investment, government capital transactions and movements of working capital and money on deposit, form the balance of payments on capital account. Taken with the current account, the overall balance of payments is a measure of funds moving into or out of the country.

These movements may add to, or reduce, the country's official reserves of gold and foreign exchange or may partly be reflected in exchange rate movements. If the authorities determine to hold exchange rates steady then they are obliged to sell foreign exchange from the reserves when the overall payments position is in deficit, and vice versa. If they are not prepared to use the reserves then the price of the currency against other currencies has to be allowed to rise or fall to the point where the supply and demand equate. This implies a change in the capital account movement on the balance of payments.

Transactions with the rest of the world have an obvious impact on the home economy. A rise in exports means more business and production for the home economy. A rise in imports can occur at the expense of the home economy. These movements, as well as the capital and money movements, can produce changes in the home economy in much the same way as changes in government fiscal and monetary policy will make a direct impact on home incomes, spending and output.

Technical changes

Finally, a new invention, new ways of doing things and new products will make an impact on the economy. The 'static' cycle shown in Diagram 1.1, of incomes, spending and production, round to incomes again, can change in a dynamic way if 'better' ways of doing things are introduced, resulting in more output for the same effort.

An economy can grow, therefore, as a result of technical innovation, though it will generally be the case that more spending power will need to be injected into the system to enable this to happen.

Social and political changes

Dynamic change also occurs in the economy as a result of social and political pressures. Social attitudes and family behaviour are constantly changing, for the most part gradually. These changes will be reflected, not only in how people spend their money but in the way they work. Working hours and holidays change and trade unions exert pressures which are reflected both at work and at the political level.

In a democracy governments are subject to powerful political pressures. The tendencies are for existing public services to be maintained and expanded and for new services to be introduced. This tendency towards expansion of the social and welfare services is interrupted from time to time, and sometimes reversed, owing to a clash of interests and resources. Governments have to balance the demands of the electorate for more public services against the need to maintain an overall balance in transactions with the rest of the world and the needs of stability (curbing inflation).

More specifically, the two main influences which force changes in government policy are unemployment and the balance of payments. Excessive unemployment results in severe political pressures making for 'expansionary' policies. A balance of payments deficit, if more than temporary, will compel a government to make restrictive changes in policy.

The cycle

It is these two main influences (described above) which lead to cyclical changes in an economy. Instead of a path of steady expansion in line with basic growth trends in the economy, there are phases of faster growth, interrupted by a slowdown (or decline) about the basic trends.

The cycles in the era since 1945 averaged around four years up to 1980. This time period was clearly determined to a large degree by the political cycle in the USA. The USA is the dominant world economy. Its main elections are at fixed four-year intervals. Thus the US political/economic cycle is a powerful influence on world trade and other national economies.

Elections in other countries are fixed in some cases and variable in others, but the average interval is close to four years. The cycles have lengthened, however. The cycles in Europe and Asia differ in timing from the USA and the various cycles within the world economy are unlikely to come together.

Growth trends

The factors which make for growth are both technical and social. It is virtually a law of economics and forecasting that all people want a higher standard of living. Few individuals are fully satisfied with their material prosperity.

The ability to raise living standards depends in the main on the proportion of the national product ploughed back both for renewal of assets and for investment in new assets. The effectiveness of managers in using existing and new assets also contributes to growth, as does the attitude of workers.

In general terms, the higher the fraction of national product ploughed back and invested, the faster the rate of growth. How much individuals are prepared to forgo out of current income to plough back in savings and investment may hinge on social and political attitudes.

Diagram 1.4   Growth and investment

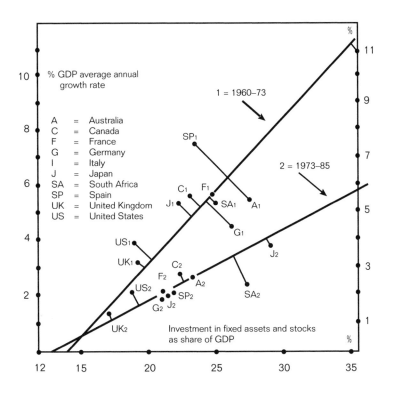

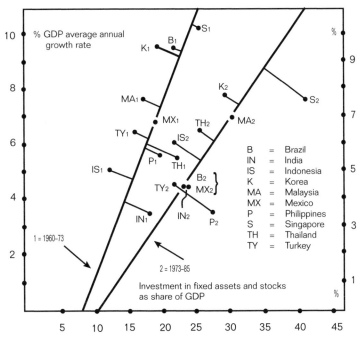

The relationship between the proportion of GDP ploughed back into new investment and the growth in the national economy (GDP) is illustrated in Diagram 1.4. The less developed economies showed faster growth records than the more mature economies. This is logical since in the poorer economies the existing stock of investment is relatively small. Thus an increment of new investment will make a proportionately bigger impact than in the richer economies.

The second feature is that investment and growth was stronger in the period 1960–73 than in the period 1973–85. This illustrates the ending in the 1970s of the post-1945 recovery and strong investment phase and the beginning of a strongly competitive phase of the world economy in which there was a growing element of surplus capacity.

It is also generally the case that the basic trends in output only change gradually because it is virtually impossible to make sudden changes in the rate of plough-back. Politicians have only limited powers to change these fundamental patterns of behaviour. The changes in basic trends from one business cycle to the next are small. Major changes take a decade or more to emerge.

The construction of a national forecast

The logical approach to compiling a national forecast is to recognize (a) the importance of the world economy (and in particular the USA) in influencing the business cycle of a specific national economy, and (b) the importance of national economic policy changes in determining the futures of individual businesses and consumers and, in turn, industrial markets.

Successful market or sector forecasting, and ultimately product forecasting, is dependent on a sound framework of broad forecasts. This framework gives a sense of perspective, outlines the constraints and limiting factors as well as the opportunities and provides an outline of the business cycle with leading indicators for the market in question.

In many cases the individual company may know more about the problems of its own customers than any outside body of forecasters. On the other hand, it is not necessarily so well informed about the overall economic situation and outlook. To construct a consistent view of the general economic environment is a lengthy and expensive operation.

Understand the data

There is a baffling problem for the layman in understanding the past as revealed in the official statistics. The figures presented to the public are based on various returns to the authorities, most of which are incomplete and subject to error. The interpretation of the background statistics is a skilled task requiring a knowledge of the likely degrees of error to be encountered. The official figures are frequently revised and allowances have to be made in order to gauge what probably happened in recent years.

In addition to the problem of interpreting national income data for years past, there is also the problem of interpreting what is happening in the present and what has happened in the recent past. There is a gap in statistical evidence between the last recorded figures and the present moment in time. This gap may be a matter of weeks or several months.

The aim of the forecast is to achieve a consistent set of estimates of practical use. Since every spending decision originates from a cash consideration, all forecasting work is designed to flow from an appraisal carried out in current money terms. In the business world profit is the ultimate yardstick and profits are judged in current prices.

Volume forecasts are essential for planning manpower requirements and capacity utilization, so that the firm requires forecasts in *both* current and constant prices (that is, volume) to obtain a complete picture of its operating environment.

In view of the uncertainties surrounding the recent past, the forecaster must use all the shreds of evidence to reach a judgement. This is similar to solving a crossword puzzle where some of the answers are known with certainty and can be used to help find the answers to other clues. The evidence from different sources such as retail sales, employment and unemployment, prices production, company profits, surveys of consumers and business confidence can all be used to establish an informed 'guess' as to the path of the economy in the recent past.

Forecasting assumptions

The starting point for any forecast has to be a set of assumptions on which to hang the sets of numbers for the components of the forecast. When running James Morrell Associates and The Henley Centre for Forecasting I held monthly meetings of our forecasting committee at which we discussed the evidence about the recent past and significant news items. We then reviewed the assumptions used in the previous month's forecast and modified these where necessary.

Major trends change slowly and the key assumptions are changed infrequently. Unforeseen changes in government policy and unforeseen shocks such as war, disruption of trade and dramatic climatic events may force a change in the underlying assumptions. The forecasts will then need to be revised.

It is important to set out the assumptions clearly at the outset so that the user may have an exact view of the features determining the forecast. The user can then ask 'what if' questions and vary the assumptions and test to see how the forecast might differ.

The assumptions for a national economy should start with a view of the world as a whole, giving the growth rate trend for the world economy and world trade. It should contain a statement about the cyclical pattern, identifying the likely good and bad years. It should then set out the features for the national economy, including the growth trend, the levels of short- and long-term interest rates, exchange rates, changes in government fiscal policy, changes in population levels and age patterns and social trends.

Political factors

In reaching agreement on the assumptions to be used for the changes in policy underlying the forecasts, it will be essential to pay close attention to politics. Not only is it necessary to appreciate the motivation of the major political parties, but it is also important to have some feel for the characteristics of the main personalities.

It is also important to have some understanding of the constitutional factors in the major countries. It is as well to know what the President of the United States of America is *able* to do, and the extent to which he depends upon the support and sanction of Congress. In other countries it is necessary to take into account the parliamentary system and to be aware of the limitations which the parliamentary timetable imposes on the government of the day. For example, the annual finance bill pre-empts a high proportion of the available annual parliamentary time, and it is always wise to remember that a parliament is unable to complete more than a limited amount of important new legislation each year.

The value of committee work in agreeing the political and economic assumptions is that the different viewpoints garnered from various corners of the economy can be reconciled and harmonized. The question of probability and timing of change can be handled with greater confidence when a number of informed opinions are brought to bear. A further advantage of the committee system is that political prejudices can be more conveniently disposed of in 'knockabout' discussion between a group of analysts, and the risk entailed through accepting the opinion of a single forecaster will be avoided.

The forecasting cycle

An outline of the forecasting cycle is shown in Diagram 1.5. The starting

Diagram 1.5 Forecasting cycle

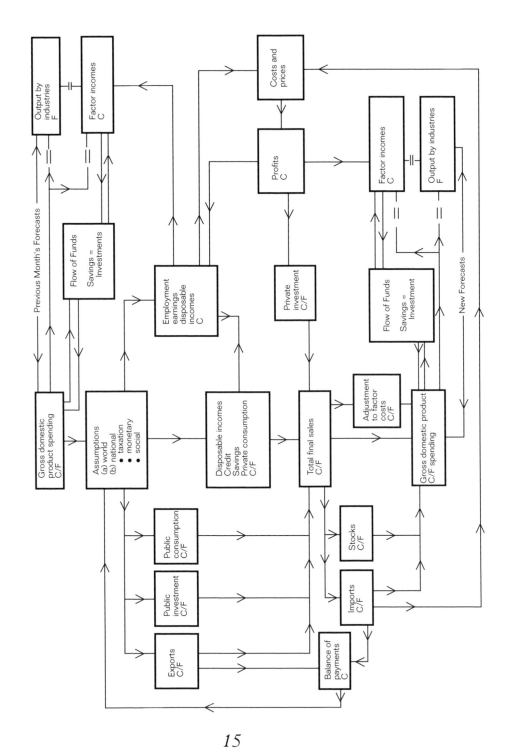

point for the cycle is at the top and is in fact the preceding forecast. In the system under review the forecasts are reconstructed at monthly intervals, and because of the short lapse of time between forecasts the previous forecast is used as the starting point for the next cycle. The assumptions, about both the world economy and national policy, are then applied to the previous forecasts and the statistical analysis begins at this point.

Some reference has been made to the question of adjusting the official statistics and filling in the gaps in recent knowledge and it is as well to consider a number of the statistical pitfalls. A great deal of time is necessarily spent on testing the validity of statistics and a general conclusion is that preference should always be given to monetary statistics, and in their raw, unprocessed state.

Price indices are in themselves artificial concepts and approximations. An adjustment from a set of figures expressed in current values to constant prices, via a price index, means that a potential source of error will have been admitted. It will be seen in consequence that volume concepts contain potential dangers. To take the example of house construction, the number of housing units started or completed in any one year is only a rough guide to the amount of work actually carried out. The content of a house will vary and there is more value added to a larger house with more rooms than average.

Seasonal adjustments, too, represent another source of potential error. Whilst it is essential to use seasonal corrections to arrive at an estimate of a trend, extreme caution must be used in interpreting all seasonally adjusted figures.

Another problem is that of homogeneity. One ton of coal is not necessarily the same as another ton. Similarly, one form of steel can be completely different from another. Houses are of different sizes, as are cars, and in nearly every instance there are problems of finding a common yardstick and standard of measurement. In the case of labour, for example, some means has to be found of comparing part-time workers with full-time workers. How does an hour of overtime work compare with an hour of normal time? Can a woman worker be compared with a man? It will be obvious, therefore, that many arbitrary assumptions have to be made in compiling background records on which the forecasts have to be constructed.

It is as well at this juncture to be warned about the temptation to use figures in such a way as to create the impression of fine degrees of accuracy. The good forecaster will adopt an attitude of extreme scepticism towards the material which he has to handle. It must be remembered that, with our present state of knowledge, we are dealing with crude approximations about the economic world. Forecasts, however, are completed in neatly rounded tables to consistent totals, with detailed figures shown down to the smallest changes. This is necessary for the completion of the exercise, but in presenting such forecasts it should be understood that it does not necessarily imply a high degree of confidence. It follows that much of the value of highly sophisticated models is lost in the unreliability of the data. Such econometric exercises must be regarded principally as learning tools. One of their most valuable by-products is the capacity to indicate where more statistical research and information is required.

Long-term trends

Before embarking upon the detail of the forecasts it is essential to establish the underlying long-term trends in the economy. Keeping in mind the forecaster's golden rule that major trends change only gradually, the task can be simplified to this extent. There are three factors on which it is important to have a clearly defined view. These are the trends in labour productivity, the determination of the price level and the balance of payments constraint. Since the size of the working population can be forecast with some degree of accuracy, an analysis of the trend in output per man will give a guide to the likely and plausible limits to the growth of total output for the economy. Labour productivity will depend in large measure upon the stock of productive capital per worker. Therefore, unless there is a dramatic change in the rate of new capital formation, the underlying productivity trend will change only gradually. The questions of labour productivity, incomes, costs, prices and balance of payments are discussed separately in subsequent chapters, but in all cases some basic trends are discernible which can be written into the overall structure of the forecasts.

Current and constant prices

Returning to Diagram 1.5, flowing from the assumptions made on both the world background and changes in government policy, the impact of these factors can be traced to the various strands of spending and demand. It will be seen from the diagram that the whole work is conducted, so far as possible, in both current and constant prices. Since spending proceeds from incomes and money, it is logical to begin the analysis from the starting point of cash available to the various sectors of the economy. All spending depends upon the availability of cash and credit.

Therefore considerable importance attaches to constructing the initial forecasts in the prices of the day. At some stage in the analysis it is possible to construct estimates of cost changes and, from the cost changes, estimates of price changes. Given a forecast of prices it is then possible to deflate the current price estimates and to reconstruct the forecasts in constant prices. Thus a second set of forecasts is obtained in volume terms and an additional means of reconciliation is available.

Incomes and spending

Diagram 1.5 shows that gross domestic product (GDP) is equated with output by industries and also by factor incomes. The major item is income from employment. Two profit totals are shown both for the public sector and for the company sector. Profits in these definitions are before deducting for depreciation and tax. The remaining components of income are rent, investment income and incomes from self-employment, such as farming, shopkeeping and professional services.

The spending estimates are constructed in two groups. Three of the items do not depend upon the model as a whole but are exogenous (originating from outside). They are not derived from automatic relationships from other parts of the estimates. These are exports, which will clearly depend upon forecasts of the world background, public investment, which will be determined by government decision, and public authorities' current expenditure, which will also be determined by political decision.

The items depending upon other parts of the model are referred to as 'endogenous' (originating from within). In the expenditure table consumers' spending, private investment, stock building, imports and the adjustment for taxes and subsidies are all derived from other relationships within the model.

The make-up of demand

The total demand on the economy is made up of exports, public sector investment and consumption (the exogenous items) plus private consumers' spending and private investment (the endogenous items). In Diagram 1.5 this total is shown as total final sales and will determine the level of stocks held in inventories.

Demand for imports will be generated in the main by total final sales and also by imports. The balance is met by home production of goods and services which comprise GDP. This figure is expressed in market prices. For some purposes it is useful to subtract indirect taxes such as excise duties, sales and value added tax, as well as subsidies. This adjusts the GDP at market prices to GDP as factor costs.

Costs and prices

From the preliminary estimates of wage incomes and output, estimates are made of the forecasts for unit labour costs. These are a major determinant of total production costs and future price developments. The forecasts of prices, when considered with the forecasts of costs, give some indication of the probable development of profit margins.

It is, of course, necessary to take into account the forecast of import prices in estimating changes in total costs. Imports are considered later in the forecasting cycle, but assumptions about import prices, derived from the forecast levels of world production and demand for commodities, are brought into the cost estimate at this stage.

Detailed forecasts and reconciliation

Up to this point the model has been constructed along macroeconomic lines. That is to say, the exercise has been carried through by examining the economy in the broadest possible terms. An alternative approach would be to construct the forecasts of the separate parts of the economy in some detail and then to add the pieces together and construct a total. In practice, it has been found that the best results have been obtained by forecasting the grand total first, breaking down the total into the appropriate sub-totals and then reconciling the parts so that they fit within the agreed totals.

When the first estimate of the GDP has been completed and revised to remove inconsistencies, estimates can be constructed in greater detail. The estimates of consumer spending and capital spending are broken down into component parts and a reconciled forecast of production by industries is prepared.

The construction of the estimates for both incomes and spending in current prices is subject to a further cross-check once the spending estimates have been deflated to allow for price increases. The expenditure table is reforecast in constant prices. Further inconsistencies can be detected at this stage and appropriate adjustments made in both the current and constant price estimates. Imports and stock building, for example, will both depend upon volume considerations as much as price factors.

At the end of the sequence of reconciliation, the final total for GDP in both current and constant prices is shown once again in Diagram 1.5 at the foot of the cycle with the three measures of incomes, spending and output as equal. But from the estimates important features will have emerged about the balance of payments. Both the export and import factors, together with the cost and price estimates, will throw new light upon balance of payments prospects. This potential situation can be checked against the original assumptions and further adjustments made in the forecasts. In practice, if the reforecasting is undertaken sufficiently frequently, the message from the forecasts about changes in balance of payments outlook will not differ greatly from one forecast to the next.

Identifying the turning points

What will emerge from forecasts constructed in this way is a picture of the changes of the economy through time, with one period influencing the next. In the forecasting system under review the forecasts run for five years ahead. In general a rough forecast is made for the horizon year for some items in order to establish an overall trend position. But the forecasts are approached by moving forward from the recent past, quarter by quarter and year by year, throughout the forecast period. In this way a clear view of the prospective business cycle is obtained. By starting from the agreed political assumptions and by incorporating the appropriate time lags in relationships between the factors and sectors, a distinct cyclical movement will be apparent for a large number of the items forecast. Within this framework certain turning points begin to be visible and the forecaster will start to identify potential changes in direction.

It will be apparent from what has been said about the unreliability of certain of the background data that extreme caution must be used in interpreting some of the forecasts. However, it will be evident from the way in which this kind of forecasting model is constructed that the numerous cross-checks applied should result in a higher degree of consistency than would be supposed by examining the degrees of error in the background statistics. For most forecasting purposes, the object is not to attain a degree of precision of plus or minus 1 or 2 per cent. Rather the decision taker wants a clear guidance on the risks involved. He will want to know whether the estimates will be valid within ranges of, say, 10 per cent. Of greater importance, he will need to know more about turning points. If the sector with which the business is concerned is about to turn downwards or to turn upwards, advance warning of the turning points will be invaluable.

A good system of forecasting should provide such warnings and, arising from the general system, illustrated in this chapter in diagrammatic form, the detail will throw up the cyclical movements of particular interest to the individual business. Much of this detail is discussed in subsequent chapters.

Conclusions

It is not necessary for the firm to forecast the national economy in the detail outlined in this chapter but the forecaster must understand the relationships described in the model. Broad forecasts for the national economy can be bought from the specialists or abstracted from press reports as shown below:

- A national forecast must take account of forecasts of the world economy and pay particular attention to the USA.

- The assumptions on which the firm's forecasts are based must be specified in detail and alternative assumptions examined to test the impact on the forecasts.
- The reliability and accuracy of the various series of figures used in compiling a forecast must be established. Use all available sources to cross-check the less reliable series.
- The national forecast is the starting point for the firm's specific forecasts for sales, marketing, investment projects, budgets and plans.

Sources

The OECD publishes country forecasts for a large number of industrial countries.

The IMF's monthly publication 'International Financial Statistics' covers all member countries and gives a wide range of background statistics.

The Economist Intelligence Unit (EIU) publishes two-year forecasts for over 180 countries.

A limited number of long-term forecasts ranging up to five years ahead are available in most of the leading industrial countries.

The European Union publishes substantial amounts of information on its member countries.

2 INTEREST RATES AND GOVERNMENT POLICY

The level of interest rates is the most important factor outside the control of the firm. Changes in short-term interest rates will affect either directly or indirectly virtually every business. The reason for this is that the great majority of businesses use bank credit to finance all or part of their working capital. Stock and work-in-progress, and in some cases the monthly payroll, are paid for from bank loan or overdraft facilities.

Thus a rising level of interest rates pushes up costs while at the same time the rising cost of credit will tend to depress sales in the credit dependent markets such as housing, motor vehicles and household durables. The overall effect is to produce a drawn-out slowing of the whole economy with an adverse effect on profits and employment.

Bank rate

Short-term interest rates are set by the country's central bank. In the leading industrial countries the central bank is independent of the government and dictates the level of rates by varying bank rate. The bank rate is the interest rate charged by the central bank to commercial banks in rediscounting bills of exchange and other bills and is part of the mechanism by which the commercial banks are supplied with cash. The bank rate, or discount rate, is the rate to which other domestic short-term rates are linked. Mortgage rates are linked, as are the rates bank and other institutions charge for loans and pay on deposits.

The whole structure of interest rates is also changed by movements in bank rate, though long-term rates tend to move in a similar direction but by smaller amounts. Bond yields and longer-term interest rates are subject to pressures in the money markets as a whole, including international markets.

Central banks

The US Federal Reserve Bank is independent of the US government and answerable to Congress in its day-to-day operations. It is, however, answerable to Congress, and its chairman reports to Congress. The bank is mandated to maintain a stable price level and to maintain full employment. It will be recognized that these twin targets are nearly impossible to meet and it would be very exceptional indeed for both targets to be met at one and the same time.

The European Central Bank (ECB), operating for the European Union, is also independent and has a target for inflation of 1 to 2 per cent per annum. It also pays great attention to the growth in the Union's money supply. The UK's Bank of England has a higher inflation target, which may well be harmonized with the ECB's target in the course of time.

In reality the central banks are not strictly independent. The managers and government bodies inevitably keep a keen eye on what is happening in both the national and world economies. They will be sensitive to the level of unemployment and profits and they will try to avoid a conflict of interest with the government of the day. Since the government appoints the head of the central bank, the bank will be aware of government policy and will try to avoid pursuing an interest rate regime which would run contrary to the thrust of government policy. The bank will also keep informed of the drift of public opinion and of the government's popularity rating.

Inflation targets

During the 1970s and 1980s, the acceleration of world price inflation, associated in part with the two oil price explosions, led to sharp increases in interest rates and extremely difficult and abnormal business conditions. Taking a long historical view through the past two centuries, those world monetary conditions must be regarded as a freak. However, that phase had the effect of strengthening the independence of central banks and of establishing the political acceptance of the need to keep price inflation under firm control.

There has been a general movement towards the adoption of low inflation rate targets and price inflation in the major industrial countries fell in the 1990s to averages of around 2 per cent per annum. Central banks have tended to change interest rates earlier so that movements in the business cycle have been smoothed out to some extent and oscillations in economic activity – spending and output – have been lessened, as have oscillations in the inflation rate.

Long phases

The long phases in the British monetary scene are illustrated in Diagram 2.1. Throughout the 19th century the world economy was dominated by the UK and the pound sterling was a world currency. The gold standard was the mechanism which regulated the national economies. Where a country ran a balance of payments surplus it gained gold. The increase in its banks' gold holdings enabled the banks to lend more, thus expanding the money supply. The domestic economy then grew at a faster pace and eventually the balance of payments would tend to move into deficit. The resulting loss of gold would force interest rates higher and the economy would slow.

Diagram 2.1   Phases in political economy, 1810–2010

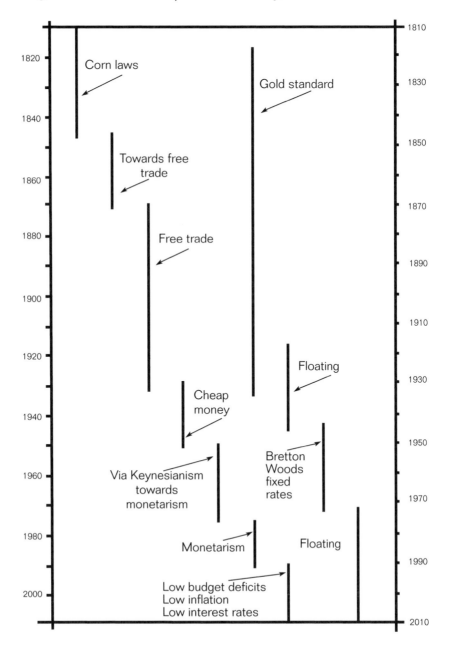

The gold standard operated for over a century until brought to an end when the USA devalued and raised the price of gold in 1934. Following the world depression, interest rates were forced down to extremely low levels and there was a period of cheap money which lasted for around 20 years. After the Second World War, governments tended to adopt Keynesian policies aimed at averting another major recession. This entailed using government fiscal policy to stimulate and regulate the economy, running budget deficits by increasing government spending.

Attention then swung towards the threat of accelerating price inflation and there was a gradual change of opinion, urged by Milton Friedman in particular, towards a monetarist approach to economic management. This entailed limiting the growth in money supply and the setting of money supply targets. If price inflation was to be averted, the growth in the money supply had to be limited to the long-term rate of growth of the economy in real terms (that is, leaving no money surplus to generate inflation).

This states the theory at its crudest and does not take account of money being used more efficiently and the speed with which money circulates, either accelerating or decelerating. In practice, raising interest rates (the price of money) tends to push up the velocity of circulation, and vice versa.

Monetarism was in vogue through much of the 1970s and 1980s, when world price inflation was exceptionally heavy. Since then national economic policies have changed, the slowing of the world economy having created surplus capacity and intense domestic and international competition. In this environment, governments concentrated on keeping the lid on inflation, curbing budget deficits and mandating central banks to use flexible interest rate policies to regulate the demand for money and limit price inflation to low levels. Inflation targets were set at levels of around 2 per cent.

It will be seen that monetary policy ran through the 20th century in phases of around 20 years and it is highly likely that this pattern will continue. This feature is of great assistance in helping to formulate longer-term forecasts of interest rates.

Control of the money supply

Short-term interest rate movements have to be seen in the context of the long-term trend. The major phase of monetary policy which began in the 1990s is focused on holding down price inflation and maintaining the value of money.

The main thrust of central bank policy has to be to limit the growth in money supply, regulating the demand for money by changing interest rates. A rate of interest is a price of money. It is a price charged for the sacrifice of purchasing power and liquidity, on the one side, and the price paid to acquire such resources, on the other. If funds are plentiful in relation to demand, rates will tend to be low, and vice versa. As a general rule, therefore, the overall level of the stock of money in the community will be of very great importance with regard to the level of interest rates.

Yet this factor, taken in isolation, tells only part of the tale. The demand for funds is of equal importance and money is required not only to facilitate normal, everyday transactions, such as household shopping, but business and commercial transactions, for both home and overseas trade, purchase of capital plant and buildings, payment of wages, payment of taxes, house purchase, dealings in the stock market and so on.

Since money has a function as a store of value, the erosion of purchasing power through inflation has some relevance for the level of interest rates. Since the rate of interest is regarded as the price for money and for sacrifice of liquidity and immediate purchasing power, any erosion in money values must be compensated in some fashion through the price of money, that is, rates of interest.

The normal tendency, therefore, is for interest rates to rise as the price level rises. Such a tendency will be distorted from time to time, depending upon the methods employed to manage the monetary situation. Over long periods, however, it is more likely that interest rates and retail prices will tend to move in the same direction. Whether or not investors have some predetermined notion of the acceptable real rate of interest, that is, the rate of interest adjusted for the changing purchasing power of money, is impossible to say. In any case, if such views are held they are unlikely to be formalized. Suffice it to say that over the past two hundred years the real rate of interest on long-term government bonds has averaged close to 3 per cent.

The increase in money supply in a capitalist system is principally driven by the growth of lending. Banks and other lending institutions generate most of their profit income from lending. Credit banking expanded from the 17th century as goldsmiths, holding customers' surplus cash, recognized that it was possible to lend out part of those deposits since there was little risk of all depositors withdrawing all their balances at one and the same time. A panic and 'run on the bank' was not impossible, however, and in 1745, for example, when the invading Stuart army reached Derby en route for London, there was a stampede to withdraw cash.

In practice, banks need to keep less than 10 per cent of customers' deposits in cash (in the till, so to speak). Part of the balance is invested in short-term government securities which can quickly be sold for cash and 70 per cent or more of customers' total deposits are lent out at higher rates of interest.

When a loan is spent the cheques issued by the borrower are paid into the banking system, raising the level of deposits. The recipient banks are then able to spend part of the additional deposits and the multiplier effects of round on round of lending create a matching rise in national deposits and the total money supply. Hence the law referred to earlier, that every advance creates it's own deposit.

If business confidence is rising, triggered perhaps by lower interest rates, good exports or tax cuts, borrowing will tend to rise. As national spending and output rise, optimism will also tend to increase. Banks will compete to lend and the upward spiral will generate faster growth in money supply, higher share prices and higher profits. Left unchecked, optimism feeds on itself and the upshot is shortage of capacity and skilled labour, rising labour costs and rising prices. Thus the natural tendency of the credit system is to magnify the rates of change in the economy, tending towards price inflation in the upswing of the cycle and towards recession and mounting unemployment in the following downturn.

Money is the vital driving force in modern society and bank lending is the major factor in increasing the money supply. The amount of cash in circulation is small compared with the total value of deposits held by banks and financial institutions and for forecasting purposes it is essential to follow the various national money supply totals.

Money supply estimates are compiled from monthly returns by banks and financial institutions. These are seldom comprehensive and the published money supply totals have a margin of error of around plus or minus 2 per cent. They are also subject to revisions. It is therefore essential to focus on the broad trends in the monthly series, rather than be swayed by individual monthly movements.

The national authorities generally publish two or more different measures of money supply. The broad measure is all-embracing and includes capital as well as current funds. The narrow measure includes cash, current accounts and deposit accounts which can be drawn down at short notice. Thus the narrow measure is a good guide to the level of funds available for day-to-day spending, whereas the broad measure encompasses investment and corporate funds used in the financing of domestic and international investment, including erratic features such as takeovers and mergers.

The central banks watch all measures of money supply and lending and will have in mind a danger point where money growth becomes too great on both the broad and narrow measures. The central bank will be inclined to raise its bank rate when money starts to grow at an 'imprudent' and inflationary pace.

Interest rate decisions

Apart from money supply, the central bank will watch and monitor a wide range of features to determine the pace of expansion and pressure on prices in the national economy. These are

- employment and unemployment;
- pay settlements and labour costs;
- commodity and import prices;
- consumer and retail prices;
- consumer credit, bank and mortgage lending;
- spending and bank clearings;
- demand and productive capacity;
- surveys of consumer and business confidence;
- production data;
- changes in fiscal policy;
- international trade and the balance of payments; and
- the exchange rate.

Most of this information is available in the financial press and it is from this web of forces that the central bank and the analyst have to construct forecasts to help reach a decision on changes in interest rates. The complexity of the economic scene makes it extremely difficult to pinpoint turning points in the business cycle with any precision. It is therefore essential to maintain charts of the historical movements in the key series and to study the pattern of previous cycles and the movement in interest rates in the context of the broad business cycle.

What should be clear from the charts is whether interest rates are in a rising or falling phase. The question then is at what level and at what point in time rates will peak or bottom out. Bands can be put around both the level and timing of the boundary point. Moving beyond that stage into the next business cycle is more difficult and, indeed, hazardous. In Diagram 2.2 the pair of charts outlining the 30-year history of UK short- and long-term interest rate movements show cyclical peaks and troughs with approximately six-year intervals. There was an exceptional break in 1992 when bank rate was sharply reduced and the pound effectively devalued from a severely overvalued level. The much lower level of base rate is associated with the lower level of price inflation established in the 1990s.

The long-term rate showed a more gradual downward trend and a less volatile profile and illustrates the importance of studying both the short- and long-term interest rate profiles.

The UK long-term rate of interest is represented by an irredeemable government bond, $2\frac{1}{2}$ per cent consolidated funds (known as 'old consols').

Diagram 2.2 Short-term and long-term interest rates

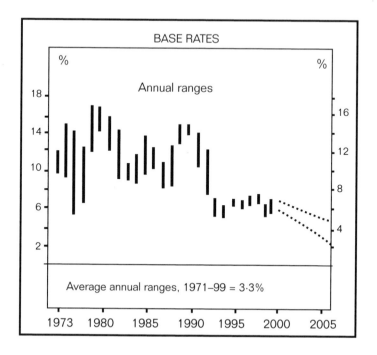

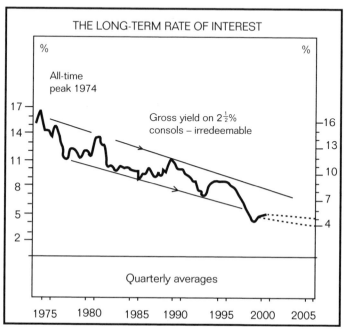

This particular issue has a near three hundred year history and is a perfect proxy for the UK long-term rate of interest. No other country has a matching currency and government bond history. In most cases currencies have been wiped out at some point by runaway inflation, as was the case with the Confederate States of the USA in the Civil War. By the same token, most countries have defaulted on occasions on their national debt.

Long-term interest rates reflect market forces and expectations and give a more significant indicator of cyclical movements than the manipulated short-term rates. Changes in interest rates must be considered in conjunction with changes in government policy in constructing a business forecast, for although fiscal and monetary policy are in most countries determined by separate bodies, both sets of policies determine the course of the modern economy.

Government policy

Up to the Second World War a government's annual budget was principally a fund-raising operation to pay for its planned expenditure. In times of war governments borrow heavily to finance the additional spending. The resulting national debt is left to future generations to refinance and pay the interest cost via taxation.

The possibility of controlling the economy through changes in taxation and spending was outlined by Keynes and others in response to the 1930s depression and from the 1940s fiscal policy has played a major role in stimulating or curbing a nation's spending power. As a guiding principle it was argued that taxation should cover public sector current spending and that capital spending, creating or acquiring assets, should be financed by the sale of government bonds. When the economy showed signs of slowing into recession it was argued that the government should offset this by putting more money into the public's pockets by a combination of increased government spending and lower taxation. The budget deficit would widen, effectively putting more money into circulation.

Conversely, governments would be advised to slow the economy when the pace of expansion became too hot by cutting government spending, raising taxation and reducing the budget deficit. In democratic regimes, however, governments tend to drag their feet over adopting a deflationary policy and in good times, when tax revenues are buoyant, there are pressures to use the extra revenue to increase government spending.

Thus fiscal policy offers another means of increasing or decreasing the money supply. But, whereas monetary and fiscal policy should be harmonized, this is difficult to achieve. Where the government has direct control of both monetary and fiscal policy its control of the money supply is likely to be inadequate, policy changes coming too late. In most cases monetary policy is exercised by an independent central bank, less sensitive to political pressures. The chances are that fiscal policy will be out of step with monetary policy since politicians pay great attention to public opinion and their electoral prospects.

US economic policy

In the USA the political constitution maintains a separation of powers. Legislation is in the hands of Congress and the federal system ensures that regional forces are strongly represented, as are the many industrial interests. The president as head of the administration is responsible for compiling a draft annual budget for presentation to Congress. For its part, the two houses of Congress prepare their own budget plans and the federal budget is ultimately agreed and passed by Congress after a lengthy period of negotiation and horse trading.

It is therefore extremely difficult to arrive at a fiscal policy tuned to smoothing the path of the economy and it must also be kept in mind that the states also raise taxes and are responsible for sizeable budgets of their own. In the 1960s, the financing of the Vietnam War overstretched the US economy. The belief that the all-powerful US economy had created a great society, big enough to provide both guns and butter, was misplaced and the result was a long series of mounting balance of payments deficits and a rising tide of national and international debt.

Tax cutting in the 1980s generated another phase of overheating and a worsening financial position. In the event, public attitudes changed and in the 1990s moved towards conservative compromises over public spending. Defence cuts in the wake of the collapse of communist regimes contributed towards a lessening of budget deficits and at the dawn of the 21st century the evidence suggested that continuing budget surpluses would lead, in time, to the extinction of the national debt. The bonus from such prudence would be revealed by the removal of the burden of interest costs from the annual budget.

The forecaster, however, will listen to the siren voices and note the political pressures for tax cuts and increases in health and education spending programmes and take a more guarded view of prospective budget changes. From this brief review it will be clear that it is unlikely that fiscal policy and monetary policy will be harmonized and it is left to the Federal Reserve to vary interest rates in an attempt to moderate the occasional excesses of fiscal policy.

The European Union

Policy in the USA moved in the 1990s towards low budget deficits and a low inflationary regime. This was part of a wider world movement and in Europe the adoption of the Maastricht Treaty bound the members of the European Union to meet a range of economic targets which included low limits to the size of budget deficits, low inflation rates and low interest rates. As argued earlier in the chapter, policy moves in long phases or fashions and it is likely that the low budget deficit regime will run for a generation or more unless broken by a major war.

In the European Union the divisions between monetary and fiscal policy are just as wide as in the USA. The European Central Bank (ECB) appears to be more independent than its US counterpart. It is more specific about its low inflation target but (so far) much more secretive about its deliberations and its targets for the growth in money supply and the exchange rate.

It is extremely difficult for the ECB to assess the Union's fiscal policy since the Union is not a federation. The Union's central budget is tiny and its governing body has little power to shape policy and to influence the course of the Union's economy.

The sovereign members of the Union retain the full powers of budget making and, although all members are constrained by the terms of the Maastricht Treaty, it is still necessary to look at the individual member countries and to make separate forecasts. The economies are not in a close cyclical alignment, just as it is unlikely that the far-flung states of the US federation are ever in an exact alignment.

Assessing political pressures

Similar differences between fiscal and monetary policy can be observed in Japan and many other countries and the forecaster can be forgiven for believing that it is impossible to predict changes in fiscal policy. Yet there are two sets of indicators which offer guidance.

The first is the programmes and manifestos of the political parties. A party which forms a government is tied, to a large extent, by the programme on which it was elected. The evidence shows that important parts of those promises are carried out. The timing of the changes and reforms may be protracted and some features may be postponed. Politicians, however, hate to be accused of breaking their promises and the forecaster should assess the election manifesto carefully to weigh up which of the policies is likely to be put into operation and when.

In the approach to an election it is necessary to study the programmes of other parties and to guess the chances of a change of government. In some countries coalitions are the order of the day and, since the formation of a coalition entails compromises, it is less difficult to forecast changes in policy.

In the fiscal field income tax is the prime revenue source. Social security taxes are of growing importance in the light of ageing populations and the demand for health services and pensions provision. Changes in corporation taxes and in social security provisions will be of particular interest to businesses, as will changes in indirect taxes such as sales tax, value added tax and excise duties.

Thus the second feature which may provide guidance to the forecaster is the permanent need of governments to raise and maintain revenues. In the case of energy taxation, for example, concern over carbon emissions and global warming, plus concern to reduce pollution, gives a strong argument for increasing taxation on the use of oil and coal fuels. A company planning a major investment in the energy sector will need to have a long-term view of prospective changes in energy taxation and tax incentives designed to influence sustainable forms of energy production, as well as fuel economy.

In other respects, although electorates welcome tax cuts, governments have little scope to cut taxes overall and where tax rates may be reduced in income tax the authorities may well offset loss of revenue from this source with increases in other areas. Across the industrialized world, total taxation is equivalent to 40 per cent of national income. It is, of course, possible to lower the total weight of taxation by transferring services provided by the public authorities to the private sector. A greater proportion of the costs of pensions, healthcare or education could be transferred to the private citizen and the forecaster must study the political scene to assess the chances of taxation being reduced by radical change and reduction of the publicly provided services.

A further feature bearing on fiscal policy arises from the differentials in tax rates between countries. Major differences in the weight of tax levied on tobacco and alcoholic drink and other consumer products create incentives for tax evasion and smuggling. The high-tax countries tend to lose home sales and tax revenues. Equally, major differences in the rate of corporation tax and capital allowances will influence companies in their decisions on where to locate.

With the progressive globalization of the world economy the scope for tax avoidance increases and the process will accelerate with the expansion of the Internet. International businesses will continually seek to find the cheapest countries in which to source their products. The net effect will be a loss of revenue to relatively high tax regime countries. The prospective worsening of the fiscal position will ultimately force those countries to lower their tax rates and to compensate by reducing the level and range of government spending.

The forecaster must therefore have a view about the likelihood and timing of changes in taxation arising from the international differences in tax rates. This levelling out will be of growing significance within the European Union, where tax harmonization has already been enforced in some areas by decision of the European Court of Justice. In the USA, too, different levels of sales tax between the individual states creates anomalies and the chances are that Internet trading will generate pressures for some harmonization of taxation.

It is necessary to take both a short-term and a long-term view of fiscal policy. In the short term the swings in the business cycle will generate swings in tax revenue sufficient to force changes on the government in framing its year-to-year budgets. Judgement on those likely changes must be tempered by an interpretation of the government's electoral promises over a longer time horizon. On a still longer time scale, in the light of long-term pressures arising from globalization of the world economy, some assessment must be made of the chances of a lowering of the general level of taxation and a gradual harmonization of tax rates and tax systems. In some major economies these changes are likely to be accompanied by a scaling down of public services and a parallel growth in private sector provision.

Wider aspects of government policy

Apart from the impact on the economy of the combined effects of changes in monetary and fiscal policy, other facets of government policy have a relevance for the national economy. The growing concern for the protection of the environment is reflected in legislation, some of which raises additional costs to business and the consumer. Apart from measures to curb atmospheric pollution and the consumption of fossil fuels, waste disposal is subject to controls and taxation. In some cases the use of packaging materials is regulated, adding to the costs of production and distribution.

In many countries legislation is in force to ensure a clean water supply and to prevent pollution of rivers and the seashore. Strict controls are enforced over food hygiene and there is a steady growth in the adoption of more rigorous health and safety regulations, all of which is reflected in business costs.

New concerns over the purity of food have arisen from the genetic modification of crops. Legislation regulating and, in some cases, banning genetic modification also has cost implications. In the rich, mature economies restrictions aimed at improving the quality of life seem certain to increase so that producers and distributors will be confronted by a gradual increase in costs over the years. The flip side of this is that consumers will have to pay more, and that spending power will, to some extent, be diminished.

In the field of employment, more and more countries will adopt a minimum wage. Hours and conditions of work have been regulated for many years.

Regulation will be strengthened in developing countries and the reduction in the length of the working week and working year, which was so pronounced through the 20th century, will continue as a world feature – again tending to raise labour costs. Social insurance provision, too, will be extended in the developing world, with additional cost implications.

Finally, anti-monopoly legislation and legislation banning the restraint of trade has a powerful effect in regulating business and is likely to be strengthened and extended in the developing economies.

Thus legal restraints and obligations must not be overlooked in appraising the prospects for changes in government policy. These add to the impact of monetary and fiscal policy in shaping the economic environment in which the business has to operate.

Conclusions

- Monetary and fiscal policy are the major determinants of the swings in the business cycle. The level of interest rates is the single most important factor outside the firm's control.
- The whole structure of interest rates is changed by movements in the central bank's discount rate (bank rate) in response to changes in spending, output, employment, the price level, balance of payments and exchange rates.
- There has been a general movement towards low inflation targets, central banks changing interest rates earlier, smoothing out the business cycle to some extent.
- Monetary policy tends to run in long phases of 20 years or so and this pattern is likely to persist.
- Money is the vital driving force in the economy. Money supply is principally driven by the growth in spending. Central banks monitor the various measures of money supply and change bank rate to control the growth of lending.
- Movements in long-term interest rates give a more significant indicator of cyclical movements than short-term rates.
- Governments can exercise some control over the economy by changing the flow of tax revenue and the levels of public sector spending, but tend to drag their feet over adopting a deflationary fiscal policy in good times, when tax revenues are buoyant.
- It is extremely difficult to arrive at a fiscal policy tuned to smoothing the path of the economy.
- Most governments in the mature industrial economies now pursue a low deficit fiscal policy and in some cases budget for surpluses.
- The forecaster must pay attention to the manifestos of the political parties as well as the economic environment in which the government has to fashion the annual budget.

- Differentials in tax rates in different countries create incentives for tax evasion as well as opportunities for corporations to relocate their operations to minimize tax liabilities.
- The progressive globalization of the world economy increases the scope for tax avoidance and the process will accelerate with the expansion of the Internet.
- The prospective worsening of the long-term fiscal position of many countries will ultimately force those countries to reduce tax rates and cut the level and range of government spending.
- Growing concern for the protection of the environment is reflected in legislation and tax policies.

Sources

Country national income accounts.

Central bank reports.

Country financial statistics.

Country budget statements and accounts.

International financial statistics (monthly from the IMF).

Party manifestos; see the national press.

OECD country reports.

3 THE GLOBAL MARKET, EXCHANGE RATES AND THE BALANCE OF PAYMENTS

It is essential for the business forecaster to take a world view of the economic environment. Since 1945 there has been a progressive expansion of world trade. Import duties have been reduced, as have other barriers to trade. As a result, international trade in goods and services has increased much faster than national income.

The global market

This change of tempo has been brought about, first, by the broadening and deepening of education in many countries and, secondly, by the expansion of international trade and the number of international corporations. There has been a substantial increase, not only in the number of universities across the world in the second half of the 20th century, but in the number of students and people acquiring academic and professional qualifications. At the same time, the number of people engaged in research has increased and university-based research is at a far higher level in relation to the size of world production in all its forms than ever before.

The same kind of expansion can be seen in the business world and a major feature of the world economy since the Second World War has been the expansion of domestic companies into giant multinational corporations. This trend has generally developed from a company's growing export business or from international trading, which then takes it to the point where it opens, or buys, manufacturing or distribution capacity in other countries. From that point the international corporation is able to introduce products and technology to and from its branches around the world. Successful research is thus exploited in the context of a world market and the speed of industrial change tends to accelerate.

Collaboration between industry and academic research departments has expanded, business commissioning and financing much of this development work. The improvement in communications has also played its part in speeding up the spread of ideas. Air travel makes it possible for individuals to meet quickly, while papers can be transmitted by fax. The Internet has also improved access to information as well as increasing the flow of discussion between individuals and groups with common interests.

The deregulation of the financial markets from the 1980s has made a major contribution towards the globalization of the world economy. There is now a vast international capital market and the flows of funds between countries has grown to very great proportions. This development has tended to strengthen the position of the multinational corporation and will contribute to the spread of new ideas and technology.

We must accept, therefore, that there is now a global economy which, in some spheres, is more powerful than national economies. This is apparent from the huge movement of capital from country to country and the relocation of production into countries with low labour costs and favourable tax regimes. The number of multinational corporations will continue to increase. The vast international capital market facilitates giant mergers and acquisitions and the concentration of economic power in the hands of big business will dominate the world scene in the foreseeable future.

It is against that background that the forecaster has to assess the pressures that determine exchange rate movements, the flow of imports and exports and the balance of payments of individual countries.

The gold standard and fixed exchange rates

The British gold standard effectively began with the fixing of the gold guinea at 21 shillings in 1717. The system evolved from day-to-day usage, bankers using guineas as part of their reserves and gold being preferred to silver by tax collectors and in domestic and international commerce.

The Bank of England ceased payments in gold in 1797, bank notes becoming legal tender. After the Napoleonic wars a parliamentary committee re-examined the currency question and the Bank of England resumed payments in gold in 1820, notes being exchangeable for gold on demand at a rate of £3.17.10½d per ounce from 1823.

The gold standard was far from being an automatic regulator since credit regulation was haphazard under the management of the privately owned Bank of England. Booms and slumps were severe throughout the 19th century and, following the suspension of the gold standard in the First World War, there was a large inflation of paper money and serious debate as to the suitability of the rigid gold standard. In the event, the UK flirted (disastrously) with the gold standard in 1926 until forced to abandon it and to devalue in 1931. The USA followed suit in 1934, and the 1930s were characterized by a period of chaotic floating exchange rates, countries seeking to protect their trading interests via competitive devaluations.

The Bretton Woods system, inaugurated after the Second World War, provided for stable and orderly exchange rate markets under the management of the International Monetary Fund (IMF). Member countries agreed to peg the foreign exchange values of their currencies, setting 'par values' in terms of gold which in turn gave 'parities' or exchange rates expressed in terms of all other member currencies. Countries further undertook not to allow their exchange rates to move more than 1 per cent above or below their par values.

Official intervention by central banks offset discrepancies between demand and supply for a currency in the foreign exchange market. In effect, each government was obliged to contain upward or downward pressure on the exchange rate by buying and selling its own currency. Intervention was financed out of a country's reserves of internationally acceptable assets: gold, national currencies exchangeable for gold and credit with the IMF.

Rather than permit competitive devaluations, as happened in the 1930s, the object was to force a country in balance of payments difficulties to correct the imbalance by making domestic adjustments, through monetary and fiscal policies. The IMF acted as a banker providing facilities to help member governments over difficult periods. In this way, countries could buy time in which to take effective, internal action to eliminate a deficit.

It was recognized, however, that in conditions of 'fundamental disequilibrium', which was never clearly defined, once-and-for-all devaluations and revaluations should be allowed. Although the system was remarkably successful for two decades, it contained structural defects which became increasingly obvious and intractable and led to its eventual downfall.

The USA emerged from the Second World War with an overwhelmingly dominant economy, including huge reserves of monetary gold. In 1950, it had record gold holdings amounting to $20 billion at the then official price of $35 per ounce. It was this huge holding which created complete confidence in the dollar and a general willingness by other countries to use the dollar as a reserve currency. Dollar holdings were more desirable than gold, since they were readily exchangeable into the metal and, at the same time, brought interest income to their holders.

However, as the dollar was the main 'intervention currency', the USA could only devalue by raising the dollar price of gold. This was considered impractical and dangerous, in that it might undermine the system and spread chaos through an undisciplined increase in monetary reserves. But as long as the dollar price of gold remained fixed, the rising cost of mining gold limited the expansion of the gold supply.

The world needed some other mechanism to get the extra international reserves to keep pace with booming world trade. The alternative was for countries to hold more dollars (or, to a lesser extent, sterling) in their reserves. This meant the USA and the UK had to run a deficit to supply the world with dollars or sterling. Ultimately, this building up of their debts was bound to undermine confidence in the value of both currencies.

One solution seemed to be to expand world liquidity further through various devices within the IMF, effectively creating new forms of international 'money' or reserves. Ultimately, special drawing rights (SDRs) were created and issued on a modest scale in the early 1970s, but these remained a relatively insignificant part of total world international reserves.

The Bretton Woods fixed rate system finally collapsed in the early 1970s as a result of the gradual erosion of world confidence in the dollar, which had, in effect, been the cornerstone of the whole system. That collapse stemmed from continuous and then massive US balance of payments deficits. These deficits flooded the rest of the world with dollars, so that the point was reached, in the early 1970s, when the world began to suffer from 'dollar indigestion'.

The cumulative deficit from 1950 to 1973 totalled $92 billion. Against this, the mounting deficits had, by the 1960s, resulted in extremely large US short-term liabilities to other countries. During the Vietnam War, the gold holding dropped to around $10 billion and it was at that point that the rest of the world began to show anxiety about the imbalance between US liabilities and reserves. Several countries began to demand conversion of their surplus dollars into gold at the official $35 price. The USA, with $10 billion in gold reserves against debts of $60 billion in other countries' reserves, decided to suspend convertibility in August 1971. The essential lynchpin of the gold exchange standard, dollar–gold convertibility, was broken.

All the major currencies were then 'floated' for the first time since the 1930s. Inevitably, there was a general appreciation of the main currencies against the dollar.

The Smithsonian agreement and the joint float

A final defence of the fixed rate system was attempted at a major international conference at the Smithsonian Institute in December 1971, where a new pattern of fixed parities was agreed. The dollar was devalued against gold (raising its price to $38 per ounce) while most other currencies were revalued. Gold convertibility, however, remained suspended.

Besides the realignment of parities, greater flexibility was introduced into the system, by allowing a wider range of fluctuations ($2\frac{1}{4}$ per cent on either side of dollar parity). But the fixed parity arrangements established by the Smithsonian agreement soon proved untenable. By February 1973 the persistence of a large deficit forced the USA to devalue again, this time by 10 per cent. The official gold price rose to $42·22 an ounce.

Fixed exchange rates were finally abandoned and most major currencies started floating. From that point flexible exchange rates became the order of the day and there is no prospect of a return to the old system of fixed parities for the foreseeable future.

Floating rates

The imbalance of the world economy in the wake of the Second World War resulted in an acute and persistent shortage of US dollars. This led many countries to impose severe exchange controls to limit the demand for foreign currency and to improve the balance of payments. These controls were gradually reduced and eliminated, so that most industrial countries now allow free international movement of funds.

The mature western economies have thus operated a floating exchange rate regime from the 1980s. Within that system the member countries of the European Common Market operated an exchange rate mechanism which limited the degree to which their rates could fluctuate. This imposed an obligation on governments to adjust monetary and fiscal policy so as to keep the currency within the defined bands. That system has been superseded with the adoption of the European common currency.

The euro thus becomes the currency which floats freely against the US dollar, yen and other currencies. Euro notes and coins replace national currencies from 2002 and other and new European Union (EU) members will convert to the euro at later dates. The size of the EU economy rivals that of the USA and the dollar, the euro and, to a lesser extent, the yen will dominate the foreign exchange markets.

It is abundantly clear from the track record of day-to-day exchange rate movements from the breakdown of the fixed rate regime in the early 1970s that exchange rate movements in the floating regime are extremely volatile. Rates have fluctuated by an average of plus or minus 10 per cent per annum from trend and an examination of currency price charts shows that exchange rate movements are highly erratic. This means that many businesses, having a substantial volume of export and import transactions, are confronted by a major forecasting problem since these normal business transactions can swing from a highly profitable to a loss-making position, having a major impact on the firm's results.

This fluctuation is illustrated in Diagram 3.1 showing the oscillations of the euro-dollar exchange rate from 1980. In the earlier years the ECU was the European unit of account and the ECU/dollar rate is used in the diagram. The movements have, on occasion, been both dramatic and alarming. The diagram also shows an estimate of the purchasing power parity (PPP) for the two currencies.

Diagram 3.1   Euro–dollar exchange rate

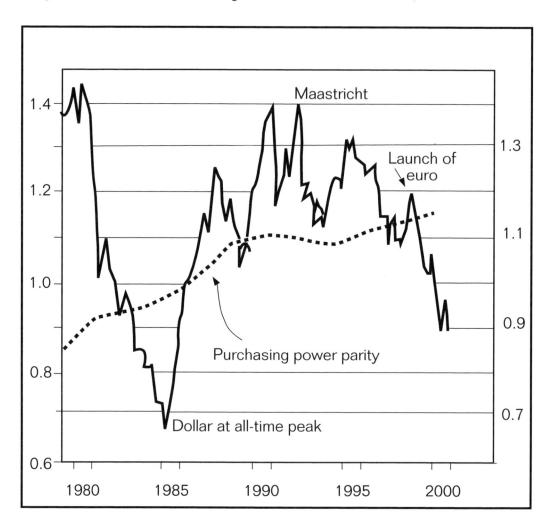

Purchasing power parity

The PPP is the estimated exchange rate at which the selling prices in the two countries are broadly equal; in other words, a representative basket of goods and services in each country would cost the same. This is a useful concept but it must be kept in mind that the measurement is to some extent subjective.

There is no difficulty in estimating year-to-year changes in relative prices since each country produces fairly reliable monthly figures showing the change in the index of consumer prices. The difficulty lies in gauging a PPP for a starting point. When were the prices in each country equal and at what exchange rate? Over a long period of time – 20 years or so – the chart of the exchange rate against the estimated PPP should show the phases when the rate is above the PPP to be roughly equal to the phases below the PPP.

This suggests that the PPP for the euro/dollar rate shown in Diagram 3.1 is perhaps 10 per cent too low. Another example is shown in Diagram 3.2. The vertical bars show the high and low points of the sterling–dollar rate for the year and, again, the diagram suggests that the estimated PPP may be a little too low. Even so, the cyclical swings and volatility of the exchange rate have been extreme, so much so that the question arises as to whether it is ever possible to make a useful prediction of exchange rate movements.

Diagram 3.2   Sterling–dollar exchange rate

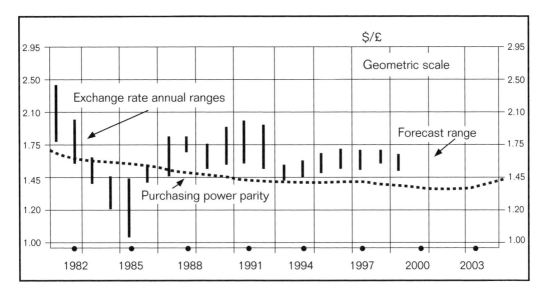

Inflation and exchange rates

Consumer price inflation can, however, be forecast with a fair degree of confidence. The trends in labour costs – the largest factor in costs – are well defined and the cyclical movements in cost and price inflation as a whole give a basis for forecasting the relative rates of price change for the main trading countries.

Where price inflation in one country exceeds that in another its currency will be worth less. Its purchasing power will decline. Thus the PPP provides a useful benchmark of value. This is well illustrated by the long series of exchange rates between currencies. The UK, with a post-1945 record of relatively high inflation, has seen sterling decline from $4·03 to $1·50 in the year 2000, indicating a rate of depreciation of 1·8 per cent per annum. Its depreciation against the German mark from its re-establishment in 1948 averaged 2·3 per cent per annum.

In these cases the evidence of the decline in sterling's purchasing power gave signals to traders which would tend to put downward pressure on sterling from time to time. Under the Bretton Woods system the government was forced to intervene, supporting the currency in the market and changing monetary and fiscal policy to curb spending and reduce price inflation. Interest rates would be forced higher and taxation increased. On two occasions sterling was devalued.

From 1971, governments were under less pressure to intervene since exchange rates could float up or down in response to imbalances of supply and demand. Even so, sharp movements could still force governments to adjust their policies. A significant appreciation of the currency will prove embarrassing since it will weaken the position of the devaluing country's traders in export markets. Conversely, a falling currency will lead to unwelcome rises in the price of imports and an increase in cost and price inflation.

Exchange rate movements, therefore, have an important bearing on domestic prices. If large enough these can be destabilizing, distorting business and generating falls in profits, unemployment and recession. Since 1971, the movements in exchange rates have been more extreme than the occasional devaluations and revaluations under the previous fixed rate regime. The bigger the movement in rates, the bigger the impact on costs and prices and the bigger the response in changes in interest rates and fiscal policy.

Thus a floating exchange rate regime tends to intensify exchange rate fluctuations. The lags between a change in the exchange rate and a change in price inflation are determined by the length of the supply chain from an imported raw material, which may have to be processed, and its movement in and out of manufacturers' stock and then into the distribution chain. Since some trade prices are on fixed contract, a change in the exchange rate can take up to a year to be reflected in retail prices. This is particularly true of exports of manufactures where price lists are more likely to be revised at yearly intervals in line with what the specific export market will bear.

The average response time is close to nine months when allowance is made for some items, such as crude oil, where a change in the exchange rate will pass through the supply chain more quickly. These lags, while existing contracts are running out, produce awkward responses in the trade balance of a country where its currency has depreciated. The volume of exports and imports will remain the same in the short term. The increase in import prices serves to inflate the import bill, while the fall in export prices will reduce export earnings. This is the 'J-curve' effect, the current account balance of payments showing a worsening followed by a larger improvement. Over the longer-term a reduction in 'inessential' imports, plus a switching to home produced goods, together with an expansion of exports, as export industries take advantage of the new opportunities in export markets, is required to make the devaluation 'work'. The J-curve effect, as noted above, takes around nine months to work itself out. This is illustrated in Diagram 3.3.

Diagram 3.3   The J curve

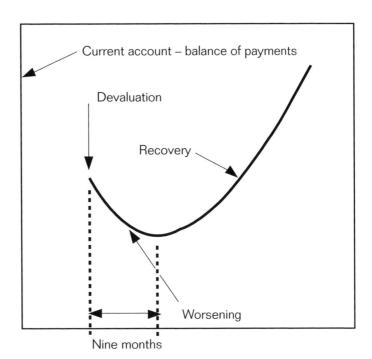

Whether or not the devaluation will improve the current account balance in the longer term depends on the behaviour of the quantities demanded of exports and imports when their prices change as a result of the exchange rate alteration. The changes in the volume of imports and exports will depend on how sensitive to price changes the demand for the goods is in the home country and within its trading partners.

For example, if a country imports necessities, raw materials and goods needed as inputs for its industries, which it does not have the resources to produce itself, a rise in the price of these goods may make little difference to the volume it imports. The effects of the oil price explosions in 1973 and 1979 on many countries' import bills provide an illustration of this point. Over the longer run the volume of oil consumption was reduced. However, most countries trade in close competition with suppliers from other countries.

There is consequently considerable scope for substitution between goods of different countries as their prices change relatively to one another.

There is substantial evidence that, in most cases, price sensitivity for both exports and imports increases over time, that export demand is more sensitive than import demand and that the combined sensitivity is sufficient for a change in the exchange rate to move the current account in the required direction. The fundamental current account factor which determines the exchange rate, in the long run, is therefore the movement of inflation between countries.

However, it is the overall balance of payments which gives the demand–supply relationship for a currency and consideration must be given to the capital account.

Interest rate differentials and capital movements

Although inflation differentials provide a logical explanation of the long-term changes in exchange rates, the differentials in short-term interest rates between countries also have a powerful bearing on rates. A country with a higher inflation rate will be obliged, sooner or later, to raise interest rates. Apart from the depressionary influence on the domestic economy, the interest rate differential will tend to pull in capital from abroad. That capital inflow may be strong enough to lift the exchange rate, offsetting the downwards pressure resulting from the higher inflation rate.

There are periods where diagrams of a pair of countries show a particularly close and direct relationship between changes in the interest rate differential and the exchange rate. It would be unwise, however, to rely upon this feature as a forecasting tool. Other capital flows can be more powerful. Sterling, for example, was transformed into a petro-currency in the 1980s, when the UK became a net exporter of oil. The soaring oil price in 1979/80 resulted in the pound being forced up to a dangerously high level, reaching $2·45. Then the dramatic fall in the price of crude oil in 1985/86 saw sterling fall close to $1·00. Such differences are absurd, leading in the first instance to a recession and six years later to a devaluation platform from which the economy expanded into a boom. Similar instances can be found in other countries where volatile commodities are a key factor in a national economy.

Political factors and the threat of war will also generate major capital movements. In 1957, the political crisis surrounding Britain's invasion of Egypt led to acute pressure on sterling. In 1962, when Russia and the USA confronted one another over the siting of nuclear missiles in Cuba, the threat of war led to downward pressure on the dollar. The 1990 Gulf War forced up the price of oil and the US dollar came under pressure.

More recently, overexpansion in the South East Asian economies and a number of major business failures and defaults resulted in sharp changes in capital flows and heavy devaluations in South Korea, Indonesia, Thailand and Malaysia. Mexico and a number of South American countries have experienced heavy flights of capital which needed major devaluations to halt and reverse the capital outflows.

Expectations also have a major influence on the exchange markets. Where a country experiences a worsening current account balance of payments and where traders can see from the monthly reports that the foreign exchange reserves are falling, the conviction will grow that the exchange rate is likely to fall. This gives an incentive for exporters to delay taking payment and importers to accelerate payment for goods to gain from the effects of a possible devaluation. These moves worsen the balance of payments still further and add to the downward pressure on the currency. In these situations expectations can lead to larger movements in capital and still greater pressures on the exchange rate. In such circumstances governments have been shown to be foolhardy in trying to avert a change which market forces have made inevitable.

The most glaring example of expectations generating massive speculation occurred in 1992, when the British government stubbornly attempted to maintain sterling at a substantially overvalued level within the European Exchange Rate Mechanism. George Soros, notably, made a very large killing at the expense of the British taxpayer by going short on sterling in the expectation that the pound had to fall. The market forces were overwhelming and the government was forced to let the pound fall and to make a heavy cut in interest rates.

A developing country will attract foreign investment where the evidence suggests that the economy can sustain an above-average rate of growth. The import of capital goods may well generate a balance of payments deficit on current account. The capital inflow, however, will support the exchange rate and, so long as confidence is maintained on the long-term growth prospects, the payments deficit may persist for long periods. The great expansion of the US economy through the 19th century was achieved with the support of a large inflow of foreign capital. The persistent current account payments deficits had led to the USA becoming the world's largest debtor nation by 1914. Thus the payments current account is not a major factor in predicting exchange rate movements and much more attention must be focused on capital movements.

The analyst is at a disadvantage, however, in that there are no up-to-the-minute data on capital movements. In any event the published national data for the balance of payments capital account are erratic, subject to major revisions and quite unreliable. The best evidence on capital movements is reflected in the exchange rate itself. Strong inflows or outflows will be instantly reflected in a rise or fall in the exchange rate. But this does not provide a basis for an exchange rate forecast. It is necessary to establish the reasons underlying the movements of capital.

The forecasting method

For business purposes it is necessary to construct forecasts for one currency against other individual currencies. Central banks construct a measure of a currency's movements by compiling an index derived from the daily exchange rates for that currency against the currencies of that country's main trading partners. These daily figures are weighted by the proportion of its trade against each of its trading partners. The index is compiled by adding all the weighted fractions of the trading partner currencies, the end result being known as the trade weighted index.

Its usefulness lies in giving a proxy for the international value of a currency and a measure of the changing competitiveness of that country's international traders. A long-term historical chart of the index will suggest levels and phases when the currency may have been under- or overvalued. When other factors, such as money supply, inflation rates, interest rates, government policy and balance of payments, are taken into account it is possible to construct a forecast of the trade weighted index and of the principal exchange rates.

THE RELATIVE RATES OF INFLATION

Cost and price forecasting are discussed in Chapter 9. For the purposes of exchange rate forecasting, it is helpful to follow the relative changes in money supply in the countries to be studied. Both the broad and narrow measures should be analysed, greater weight being given to changes in the narrow measure since this is more relevant to future changes in price inflation.

Where the money supply is rising faster than the national income the 'surplus' money will tend to accelerate spending and push up prices at a faster rate. If money growth is faster in relation to national income in one country than another, purchasing power will decrease faster and the currency will tend to fall. The money indicator therefore gives a guide to the likely short-term movement in the exchange rate. This should be checked for constructing cost and price forecasts for each country, working from the changes in labour costs, material and import prices, plus allowances for changes in interest rate costs and government policy. These forecasts should be projected into a longer-term forecast. The consumer price index or retail price index should be used as a proxy for price inflation because these are a fair proxy for the goods and services which feature in international transactions.

The relative movements in prices between one country and another can then be used to estimate the changes in the purchasing power parity (discussed above). The PPP does not provide a prediction of where the exchange rate will settle. What is evident from the historical records is that the higher or lower the exchange rate moves from its estimated PPP, the greater the chance that it will change direction and move towards the PPP level.

Some further guidance can also be found by measuring the deviation over time of the exchange rate from the PPP. These differences, when plotted on a chart quarter by quarter, highlight the cyclical swings in the exchange rate. Past patterns give indications of the timing and duration of past deviations, which can then be used in projecting the exchange rate forecast.

THE INTEREST RATE DIFFERENTIAL

The differences in short-term interest rates between countries can be calculated and plotted in a similar way and compared with the movements in the exchange rate. For some periods the changes in the two series will be nearly identical. Where the series diverge, other forces are more powerful and large movements of capital will push the exchange rate beyond the level indicated by the interest rate differential.

Those capital movements will be influenced by expectations of changes in the exchange rate and by changes in the volumes of both direct and portfolio investment. Where businesses in one country increase or decrease the flow of investment into another country on a large scale, those movements may have a greater impact on the exchange rate than the interest rate differential. Large takeovers and acquisitions, or large injections of new capital into a foreign subsidiary, will generate abnormal capital flows.

Yet the interest rate differential is still an important factor in the exchange rate equation since it encapsulates central bank policy responses to the changing economic scene and the *anticipated* changes in the economy bearing on spending, output, inflation and the balance of payments.

GOVERNMENT POLICY AND THE BALANCE OF PAYMENTS

The government and the central bank take note of the monthly trade figures covering exports and imports and the other items which make up the current account of the country's international balance of payments. By and large, the authorities do not like to see deficits, and a curious feature of the international statistics is that, when the payments figures for all the countries in the world economy are added together, they invariably show a world balance of payments deficit. This is, of course, impossible and it illustrates that national balance of payments statistics contain a 'cautious' bias, tending to depress the balance. This must be taken as a warning that the payments figures are far from dependable, except where the balances are large. Nevertheless, traders and dealers watch the published figures and act on them, regardless of their accuracy. As in all markets, *it is what people believe that counts*, even where this turns out to be at odds with the hard facts.

A country's trade prospects will depend not only on the rate of growth of world markets but on its exchange rate and costs and prices relative to the international markets. If its currency is undervalued it will have the opportunity to expand its exports more rapidly and to curb imports. The balance of payments will therefore 'improve' and will ultimately lead to a strengthening of its exchange rate, provided the trade performance is maintained.

The forecaster must make allowances for changes in government policy in response to the country's balance of payments position and the value of its currency. Where the problems are acute and a payments deficit is of daunting proportions, the country can borrow from the IMF. Where major financing is required the IMF will lay down conditions for the loan, dictating changes in government policy which may impose fundamental reforms. In most cases the rescue operations have been successful, restoring confidence in the currency and a recovery in the exchange rate.

Exchange rate risks

When the problems of measurement, and the weakness of some of the relevant data are considered, it will be seen that exchange rate movements can be, and often are, capricious. Volatile exchange rates comprise a risk to the business in its international transactions and it follows that exchange rate forecasting is equally risky.

It is possible to offset some of the risk by using the forward market to cover exchange rate transactions. However, it must be remembered that, although it is possible to buy insurance cover for most contingencies, that cover comes at a price. Where the uncertainty is great, as it must be in a floating exchange rate regime over longer time periods, the insurance cover must be costly and is therefore sometimes impracticable.

Against that background it is prudent to establish a discipline for handling the firm's exchange rate transactions and forecasts. For example:

- Reduce exposure and risk by matching purchases and sales of a currency where possible.
- Use the forward market.
- Invoice in the currency of the market you are selling into where practicable and move your selling prices in line with price movements in that market at intervals acceptable to that market.
- Use the price forecast for that country as a guide to fixing your own selling prices.

- Use the cost/price forecasts for the country in question in conjunction with the price forecasts for the export market in question to establish the profitability of that market at the forecast exchange rate.
- Then ask the question: What will be the effect if the rate is plus or minus 10 per cent different from the central exchange rate forecast, and assess risk accordingly, asking – can you cut costs and improve your product's marketability? Should you stay in that market?
- Equally, ask the question: Can you win business from the importer, bearing in mind that he will inevitably have higher transport costs to absorb?
- Finally, keep in mind that there is a strong chance that exchange rates will fluctuate by as much as 10 per cent either side of the general trend in the course of a year, and sometimes more.
- This means that, even if the trend is predicted exactly, there is a chance that the rate on any particular day will be up to 10 per cent away from trend. Therefore the risks in playing the market are large.

Conclusions

- There is now a global economy made up of multinational corporations which in some spheres is more powerful than national economies. The concentration of economic power in the hands of big business will continue to increase.
- In the floating exchange rate regime rates have fluctuated by an average of plus or minus 10 per cent per annum from trend. Businesses are therefore confronted by a major forecasting problem with their international transactions.
- The purchasing power parity (PPP) between a pair of currencies is a useful benchmark for detecting when a currency is under- or overvalued.
- Where price inflation in one country exceeds that in another, its currency will be worth less and its PPP will decline.
- Exchange rate movements have an important bearing on domestic prices. The bigger the movement in rates, the bigger the impact on costs and prices, and the bigger the response in changes in interest rates and fiscal policy.
- The differentials in short-term interest rates between countries have a powerful bearing on exchange rates via international capital flows.
- Expectations have a major influence on the exchange markets. These are reflected in movements of capital which can be of very large proportions, swamping the effects of the balance of payments on current account.
- The relative change in prices between one country and another is a key factor in exchange rate forecasting. Deviations from an exchange rate from its PPP highlight the cyclical swings.
- Volatile exchange rates comprise a risk to the business community. Exchange rate forecasting is equally risky. Although it is possible to buy insurance cover for most contingencies, that cover comes at a price which in some cases becomes impracticable.

Sources

International Financial Statistics (monthly from the IMF).

See national statistical sources for data on prices, interest rates, balance of payments and exchange rates.

The *Currency Forecaster*, published monthly by the Informa Publishing Group, gives forecasts of nearly 50 exchange rates for the short term and up to five years ahead, plus other related data and forecasts. It is compiled in New York to give 'consensus' forecasts from 80 collaborating firms around the world.

4 GLOBAL WARMING, ENERGY AND COMMODITY PRICES

The world's climate has always been erratic. Recent evidence, however, suggests it is becoming more volatile, and scarcely a week passes without news of a climatic disaster somewhere in the world. A number of industries are closely affected by climate change, notably insurance, planning and development and agriculture. Other sectors are indirectly affected and there is a need for long-term forecasts of climatic fluctuations as well as for week-to-week forecasts.

We are now in a climatic warming phase, with average world temperatures increasing through the 20th century. Between 1900 and 1940, temperatures rose by 0·4°C, following a relatively cold period, and then fell. But from 1980 the rise in temperatures has resumed, the increase almost certainly arising from man-made global warming.

This development has focused attention on the long-term history of the climate in an attempt to understand all the causes of changes in world weather conditions. Governments have allocated large sums for research and there is substantial collaboration between scientists and meteorologists in the attempt to measure and interpret the enormous complexities of the earth's climate (see Diagram 4.1).

In the absence of comprehensive measurements from all parts of the globe of temperatures, barometric pressures, wind speeds and ocean currents, we have remained extremely ignorant of weather history. However, the advent of spy satellites and expanding computer capacity are helping to fill the great gaps in our knowledge and one certainty for the 21st century is that there will be a dramatic advance in our understanding of the climate.

Global warming

Carbon dioxide emissions have been increasing from the onset of the Industrial Revolution in the 18th century. The use of coal in making iron and steam power and the continuous expansion of industrial production has resulted in a gradual build-up of CO_2 in the earth's atmosphere. The burning of fossil fuels in electricity production and in motor transport has raised the level of carbon emissions much faster. Whereas CO_2 made up 0·028 per cent of the atmosphere at the beginning of the 19th century, the fraction has risen by a quarter to 0·035 per cent.

Diagram 4.1 Global temperature variations

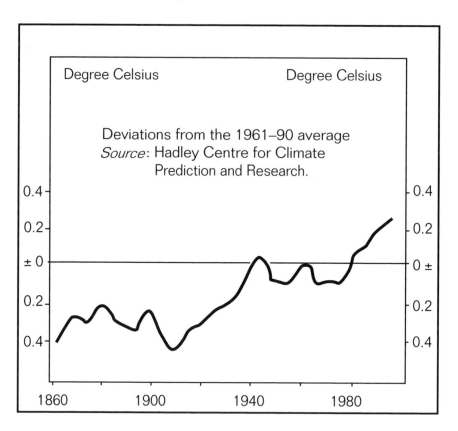

Carbon dioxide is absorbed by the oceans and by plants. Thus the increase in CO_2 in the atmosphere has been brought about by the rise in man-made carbon emissions going beyond the capacity of the natural environment to absorb the surplus. That growing fraction of CO_2 in the atmosphere sits like a blanket around the globe which prevents the warmth reaching us as sunlight from being radiated away. CO_2 molecules are good at absorbing heat, as are methane, produced by animals, and the CFCs used in sprays.

Sunspots and volcanoes

Apart from a variety of very long-term climatic cycles, or rhythms, there are shorter oscillations. The shortest of these, with 11-year cycles, is caused by variations in the sun's brightness associated with the sunspot activity. The level of sunlight reaching the earth drops by no more than 0·1 per cent, but this is still sufficient to disturb weather patterns and reduce crop yields to some extent. Curiously, observers reported low levels of sunspots in the Little Ice Age of the 17th century. In that period ice fairs were held on the Thames. The Little Ice Age lasted from the 13th to the end of the 19th century and the average temperature in Europe was probably 1°C lower than in the latter part of the 20th century.

Climate is also affected by volcanic activity. Every 8·85 years the orbits of the sun and moon coincide, creating exceptional high tides. The combined weight of water and friction can bear on sensitive coastal areas, triggering earthquakes and volcanic eruptions.

A volcanic eruption hurls dust and sulphuric acid 20 miles into the stratosphere. The resultant dust cloud blots out the sunlight and disperses round the world, reflecting sunlight away from the earth, back into space. The sulphur dioxide is converted into sulphuric acid aerosols and these tiny particles remain in the stratosphere for several years.

Not only do volcanoes cause a general cooling of the global climate, but they also distort weather patterns, with adverse effects on agriculture and crop yields. Records of volcanic activity can be traced back over many centuries. There was a massive eruption of Laki in Iceland in July 1783 which led Benjamin Franklin to conclude that the cold winter of 1783/84 in Northern Europe was caused by the dust from the volcano. In 1815, the eruption of Tambora in Indonesia, which is estimated to have ejected five to ten times as much sulphur as Pinatubo – the biggest eruption of the 20th century – was followed in 1816 by the 'year without a summer' which brought June frosts to New England and the latest wine harvests since records began in 1482.

The eruption of Krakatau in 1883 was the second largest in the 19th century, killing over 30 000 people in Java directly from a huge tidal wave. Pinatubo in the Philippines erupted in 1991 and affected weather patterns in the following two years.

Volcanic activity is likely to be at its maximum in the current cycle around 2010, with the peaking of high tidal forces. The period from 1940 to 2010 is one of increasing volcanic activity, having a cooling effect on the world's climate. Against that background the rise in average temperatures must be seen as attributable to the man-made greenhouse effect.

The climatic evidence

On balance, the evidence still seems to confirm that temperatures are rising, particularly when account is taken of the shrinkage of the polar icecaps. The reserves of glacial ice around the world are melting more quickly than has previously been suspected. The Alps have lost around a half of their ice in the past century. In Spain the number of glaciers has shrunk from 27 to 13 since 1980. The ice rivers of the Tien Shan mountain range on the Sino-Russian border have lost 22 per cent of their ice volume since the 1950s, whilst the glaciers on Mount Kilimanjaro in Kenya have shrunk by a quarter.

The rate of warming is greater than at any time in the last six centuries and the scale of the retreat of the glaciers is probably unprecedented. Although glacial melting has made only a slight contribution to raising sea levels this effect is likely to increase since melting is leading to an increased flow of some rivers. The long-term forecasts by the International Panel on Climate Change suggest that sea levels will rise by as much as half a metre by 2100, a third of the change coming from run-off from melting glaciers and icecaps and more than half from the thermal expansion of the oceans as they warm up.

More recent research based on satellite studies indicates that sea levels are likely to rise faster than previously suggested. Over the past century thermal expansion of the oceans and melting mountain glaciers have played a far greater role in raising sea levels than the melting of the Antarctic.

The scientific consensus on global warming is steadily increasing and it is likely that governments will adopt still tougher targets for the limitation and reduction of carbon emissions. Even so, there will still be a significant time lag – perhaps as long as 50 years – before effective measures begin to show results.

Climatic change and its consequences

The wider consequences of climatic change are extremely difficult to predict at this stage. What is far more certain is that complex computer models of the world's climate will be continuously expanded through the next 30 years to the point where the changes in temperature and rainfall in the various regions of the world will be predicted with a fair degree of confidence.

What seems likely is that man will not respond quickly enough to limit global warming by cutting energy consumption and carbon emissions. As a result, global temperatures will probably rise by between 1° and 3°C by the year 2100. The melting of glaciers and parts of the polar icecaps will raise sea levels, while the raising of temperatures will have profound effects on wind and rain patterns and on all forms of animal life and vegetation.

Over the years the awareness of climatic change and its effects will lead to widening concern and there is therefore every likelihood that governments will come under pressure during the 21st century to initiate policies aimed at *cutting* carbon emissions. There will also be pressures to take defensive measures to prevent flooding, such as those undertaken in the Netherlands over the centuries and particularly since the catastrophic flooding in 1952.

The world insurance industry has accepted increasing climatic disturbance as evidence of global warming. The cost of insurance cover for climatic disasters will continue to rise and this will be part of the economic cost to be faced by society through the 21st century.

Further disturbing evidence of change is the increase in the number of icebergs originating from Greenland's glaciers. The icebergs drift southwards into the west Atlantic off Labrador in the cold current which meets the Gulf Stream. The increasing movement of the glaciers is further evidence of global warming and a progressive increase in warming through the 21st century raises the prospect of a strengthening of the movement of cold water to the south, off the eastern American seaboard. A change of that magnitude could gradually change the path of the Gulf Stream, weakening its warming effect on north west Europe, with a dramatic effect on climate.

Economic pressures bearing on food production resulting from changes in temperature and rainfall will result in far-reaching adjustments, including movements in populations. Famines will drive millions of people to migrate, causing acute political problems where other countries are unwilling to accept refugees.

Warming also poses a major economic problem through the gradual melting of Arctic areas of permafrost. There is a vast network of engineering installations for oil and gas extraction in those regions which would suffer very great damage as the frost thawed. In addition, areas where the land is already subsiding because of extraction of oil or water would be particularly hard hit and this includes Venice, Tokyo, parts of south Texas and Bangkok. Abu Dhabi and Dubai will also be vulnerable and the salt flats in the Arabian Gulf would be transformed into lagoons.

The rise in temperature will result in the migration of the forests encircling the northern hemisphere up to 700 km to the north. Although large numbers of people would not be involved, the timber industries would be affected, forcing the relocation of population and industry.

The consequence for agriculture and food production of global warming will be far more profound. The computer analysis and predictions of regional climatic change will generate more confident warnings through the next 20 years. From what we know at this moment it seems likely that the American Mid-West – the great grain producing area – will become a dust bowl, while vast areas of Russia will be capable of increasing grain output.

Should changes in rainfall patterns damage food production in both China and India, the consequences would be extremely grave. Those two countries account for 40 per cent of the world's population and it seems unlikely that the rest of the world would be capable of making good the food deficit in the short run. Famine and large-scale migration would provoke international disputes, possibly leading to war. Given time, however, economic solutions could be found, food production being raised in other countries and the patterns of trade and payments adjusted to meet the shortages.

El Niño

Another feature of the world's climate which will receive increasing attention is the periodic warming of the Pacific Ocean off the western coast of South America which has been given the name 'El Niño' – the Christ Child. The name derives from the timing of the arrival of the warm water first observed around the Christmas period.

El Niño occurs at roughly five-year intervals, lasting for about 18 months, and is powerful enough to disrupt the world's climate. It is not yet known what triggers its appearance or influences its strength. The surface water off Peru is warmed by several degrees, covering an area equivalent to twice the size of the United States. The fish that normally inhabit the area retreat and warm water species replace them.

The warmer water moves across the Pacific from west to east, contrary to the normal patterns. As a result there is cooling of the waters and a drop in rainfall affecting Australia, the Indonesian archipelago and Southern Africa. The warm water arriving off South America generates an increase in rainfall and flooding in California and the south of the USA as well as Peru and other areas of the central American coast.

Drought conditions have worsened and the 1997/98 El Niño was the most severe of the 20th century, surpassing that of 1982/83 which claimed nearly 2000 lives and damaged crops and property worth $13 billion. The sea temperature off the tropical Pacific rose by 5°C above normal in 1997 and the severity of the droughts in eastern Australia, southern Africa, Indonesia and the Philippines raises concern about the viability of agriculture and life in those areas.

There are fears that the El Niño phenomena will occur at shorter intervals and with greater force and it is believed that this change in pattern and effect is linked to global warming.

The impact on industry

The increasing volatility of the world's climate, leading to more natural disasters and damage to property and crops, will force up the costs of insurance. Thus both businesses and households should build higher insurance costs into their forecasts.

The rise in sea levels, already affecting some areas, will put low-lying areas around coasts and rivers at risk of inundation. Coastal erosion will tend to increase as storms become more frequent and dramatic. Development plans for areas at risk have to be tested to assess the chances of damage and destruction over the life of any potential construction project. Prospective buyers or tenants will be increasingly aware over time of the risks, and property values will be affected. Planners and developers therefore need to construct long-term forecasts of the likelihood and extent of the effects of rising sea levels.

For forecasting purposes, the reports from the International Panel on Climate Change (IPCC), the body that advises the United Nations on the climate, will give increasingly confident predictions of the effect of climate change on regions. In addition, individual countries will produce studies of the impact. The Netherlands, with large areas of land below sea level, has been well to the fore in preparing for the problems and many other countries will publish studies of the domestic implication of rising sea levels for their territories. Firms, where the problems may be relevant to their business, should take full account of such forecasts.

Agriculture will be affected in a number of ways. Climate change apart, the growth in world populations and the industrialization of developing countries will raise demand for supplies of fresh water. Many countries will be confronted by water shortage. Agricultural irrigation is responsible for large consumption of water and in some regions practices will have to be changed.

Climate change will shift the patterns of rainfall and important food-producing regions, such as the US grain belt, will become increasingly arid. The problem cannot be solved by irrigation. Moreover, areas such as this will also suffer from increasing loss of soil fertility. The world is therefore faced with the likely decline of food production in some areas.

Global warming will lead to other areas becoming more productive, though the opening up to agriculture will require substantial investment. Yet warming produces other hazards and insects have already migrated, following the temperature changes. This will increase the incidence of disease, damaging crops and livestock as well as human beings.

Agricultural investment must take account of the long-term forecasts of climate change. Farmers, of course, must take note of day-to-day changes in weather and, in temperate climates, where seasonal weather patterns can be erratic, the farmer needs short-term forecasts to help determine when to work the land, to plant and sow and to harvest. Weather forecasts for up to a week ahead have become more dependable and in many countries farmers have access to regional and even local forecasts to help plan their day-to-day operations.

From the consumer industries' point of view, short-term weather changes can make a sharp impact on sales. Sales of drinks, ice cream and certain foods are affected by variations in temperature and the short-term weather forecasts are critically important to the production and distribution of those products. In this respect it is essential for those businesses to keep a day-to-day diary so that it is possible to compare weather conditions and sales for comparable dates in previous years. All businesses should maintain diaries so that special events which affect the business (but may be soon forgotten) can be recalled to help analyse sales results.

The implications for the energy industries

Climate change has deep implications for both the producers and the consumers of energy. Production and distribution of energy require vast investments and in many cases these investments will have long potential life spans. It is therefore necessary to compile long-term forecasts and these must take account of legislation and tax changes bearing on the production and consumption of the various forms of energy.

The concern to reduce carbon emissions focuses attention on the relative costs of various fuels. Intensive research into the development of an economical electric-powered motor vehicle is likely to result in the displacement of petrol-fuelled cars at some point in the future. That change is likely to be gradual rather than sudden. Allowance has to be made for the continuous improvement in engine technology and efficiency of the petrol-driven car. Its carbon emissions will decrease with the improvement in fuel economy and this trend will delay the erosion of the car market by electric-powered vehicles.

The defensive factors in an industry are often overlooked and a comparison of the efficiency of the steam power of the first locomotives in the 19th century and the modern counterpart shows a dramatic and sustained improvement over a period of nearly 200 years. Swiss engineers have developed steam locomotives which are as efficient as their electric or diesel-powered counterparts.

Thus energy investment projects have to be analysed with an eye to technical advances in competing fields as well as the changes in direct costs imposed by the costs of crude fuel and taxation. The forecasts take on a different complexion for different parts of the world. In areas where the geological strata are favourable coal is cheap to mine. In those cases transport to the consumer may cost more than the mining costs. Where coal deposits are close to centres of population, coal-fired power stations may be cheaper than gas or oil-fired plants. Conversely, in some oil-producing regions the cost of crude oil is so low that no other fuel can compete.

Climate changes, however, cannot be left out of the equation in any long-term energy forecast. Some assumptions have to be made about the gradual increase in the supplies of renewable energy – of wind power, solar power, water power and thermal power. It is also necessary to take account of the development of hydrogen as a virtually limitless power source.

Nuclear power, once the great hope for an alternative clean source of energy, has proved to have high short- and long-term risks of radioactive contamination. The Chernobyl disaster was a gruesome reminder of a potential danger of nuclear accidents. The growth in the number of reactors worldwide increases that risk. The greater risk, however, lies in the problem of ensuring the safe disposal of nuclear waste and in the decommissioning of old and redundant nuclear power units. Nuclear waste can remain radioactive for centuries and the provision of 'safe' disposal and storage of the highly poisonous material adds to the true costs of nuclear energy. Nuclear energy is now uncompetitive and it is plainly uneconomic to commission the building of new capacity unless there is to be a major increase in the cost of other sources of electricity.

The energy prospects for the 21st century are, nevertheless, relatively promising in that we are on the verge of an economic breakthrough in both solar and wind energy production. Beyond that, underwater methane gas, biomass, the solar cell, nuclear fusion and liquid hydrogen may all offer alternative economic sources of relatively clean energy by the end of the 21st century.

The cost of solar thermal electricity has fallen substantially, to the point where in some regions it can compete on costs with conventional fuels. Photovoltaic (PV) cells which are semiconductor devices generating electricity directly from sunlight were first used in the 1950s to power space stations. These now bring power to large populations in poor countries such as Kenya, Brazil and South Africa, often without a subsidy. Technical improvement combined with economies of scale have cut the costs of the modules of PV cells to a fiftieth of what they were in the 1970s. Even so, electricity generated from PVs is still far more costly than that produced from a fossil fuel power station. Where solar energy scores is in its low cost of distribution compared with the high costs of distribution via electricity grids from the power stations. In Kenya, more households get power from the sun than from the national grid.

Wind power is also close to price equality with fossil fuels, with the advantage of lower distribution costs. Wind plants can take less than a year to build, compared with ten years or more for nuclear plants, and although winds may fail on some occasions through the year, provided the plants are connected to a grid and contribute less than around 20 per cent of the total power generation, the electric utilities can cope with fluctuating supply, just as they manage wild swings in hourly demand. Other technologies are also being developed to store energy so as to smooth the changes in supply and these may well become economic and effective by mid-century.

Shell, which has long used scenario forecasts as an aid to planning, suggests that renewables, such as sun and wind power could be meeting more than half of the world's energy demand by 2060. The World Bank is searching for suitable sites in China and India for both wind and PV plants which can be operated without subsidy. Looking further ahead, further technological improvements and the mounting economies of scale (more equals cheaper) make it fairly certain that these sources will account for an increasing share of world energy consumption.

The long transition

Given time, therefore, carbon emissions will be reduced and global warming halted. This still remains a distant prospect simply because so little is being spent on research and development of renewables compared with spending on nuclear and hydro power. According to the International Energy Agency (IEA) rich country governments spend over half their $8 billion a year energy research budgets on nuclear programmes and only 10 per cent on renewables. Poor countries (excluding the former communist bloc) already generate nearly 5 per cent of their electricity from nuclear or hydro power and only 0·3 per cent from renewables. They are building large numbers of new nuclear and hydro plants.

The World Bank stresses that nuclear power cannot compete with fossil fuels once the cost of dealing with spent fuel and decommissioning are taken into account. Thus, given their present cost advantages, fossil fuels will continue to provide the lion's share of the world's energy. The world will therefore become more polluted, particularly since China and India will meet such a large part of their industrial and consumer energy demands from fossil fuels.

The disparity in energy consumption per head of population is so great between the USA at one extreme and the populous developing countries at the other that no one can doubt the potential growth in world energy demand. The IEA suggests that energy consumption in the rich countries that make up the OECD will grow by an average of no more than 1·3 per cent per annum across the first decade of the 21st century, whereas consumption in the developing countries will average 4·2 per cent. These numbers are clearly in the right ball park. Rigorous economies in the western world – should they be achieved – will be overwhelmed by the burgeoning growth in demand in the developing countries. Not until the effects in pollution, carbon emissions and global warming are substantially greater than at the outset of the new century will policies and practices be adjusted sufficiently to accelerate the displacement of fossil fuel energy by renewable sources. That phase will probably unfold in the second quarter of the century.

On the immediate horizon, the *fuel cell* will become an economic proposition early in the century. A fuel cell is a special type of battery which does *not* contain stored chemicals. The reactants that deliver electric power are fed continuously into the cell and the cell will continue running for as long as the reactants are fed in. On-board fuel storage gives the cell a greater range than the battery-powered car and takes much less time to refuel.

The first fuel cell was demonstrated as long ago as 1839 and left on the shelf until the 1960s, when it was used for powering spacecraft and other specialized tasks. There is now widespread research in progress in the USA, Japan and Europe aimed at harnessing a liquid fuel, such as methanol, to the fuel cell via a reformer, to run the cell on hydrogen. Chrysler, in partnership with others, is working on a cell running directly on petrol to power an electric car. Chrysler estimates that a fuel cell would use petrol 50 per cent more efficiently than a conventional internal combustion engine. This would cut polluting emissions by as much as 90 per cent.

The cell will have other applications than in transport, and in the field of stationary electric power generation there is very wide potential demand from customers such as small communities, hospitals, hotels and business premises for small generating units. This will eventually reduce dependence on the electric grids and make further contributions to the reduction in pollution and dependence on fossil fuels.

The forecaster in this field must therefore take account of a wide range of technical changes as well as the political and fiscal changes which will determine the relative cost as well as the absolute cost of energy production and consumption. These factors will vary from country to country according to economic geography and the differences in political approach.

The cost of commodities

The majority of manufacturing businesses buy commodities directly or indirectly. Materials and components used in the manufacture of its products will incorporate raw or processed materials. The cost of these inputs can be substantial and it is therefore necessary to forecast the relevant commodity prices so as to compile a cost profile for the manufacture of the final product.

In the jargon of the commodity markets, agricultural products are known as 'soft' as opposed to the metals. The softs are obviously sensitive to climatic conditions. Thus Brazilian coffee prices, for example, can move dramatically if frosts damage, or threaten to damage, the potential crop. Any shortfall in crop yield in the soft commodities will push prices up, whilst bumper harvests generally depress the market.

The food products traded in the commodity markets and included in the *Economist*'s weekly price index are the following:

- wheat
- coffee
- sugar
- maize
- soyabeans

- rice
- soyabean meal
- beef American and beef Australian.

Wheat, coffee, sugar and maize are the more important items. Other crops and animal products are traded in the commodity markets and in the USA these include orange juice, pork bellies and a wide variety of items stemming from a continental farming industry.

The non-food agricultural commodities included in the index are:

- cotton
- timber
- hides
- rubber
- wool 64s and 48s
- palm oil
- coconut oil
- soyabeans
- soyabean oil.

Cotton is by far the most important item.

The base metal products are listed in the index, but not the precious metals. Gold, silver, platinum and other rare metals are also traded as commodities. The metals included in the *Economist* index are:

- aluminium
- copper
- nickel
- zinc
- tin
- lead.

Aluminium and copper are the most important of the metal commodities.

The overall index provides a barometer of world demand. Most of the trade is priced in US dollars and economic activity in the USA is the dominant force in world markets. For the purposes of forecasting, the index gives a picture of the broad changes in supply and demand. Shortages logically force up prices. Above-average rises in demand may tend to create shortages, forcing prices higher. A historical chart of the index will, therefore, illustrate the major cyclical movements – the good times and the bad times – and those patterns will give some guidance on the timing and range of the next cycle. The *Economist* index has a continuous history from its inception in 1864.

Energy prices are not included in the *Economist* index. The various categories of oil and gas are heavily traded and there is some logic in separating energy costs from the broad spectrum of commodity costs.

The firm, however, will be interested in specific commodities, most of which are subject to substantial price movements. In the markets, the biggest being Chicago, commodities are traded for future delivery as well as for spot (immediate delivery). There is a large element of speculation in the day-to-day trading and there can be significant movements during trading hours in immediate response to news items and rumours. The speculator, dealing in futures, does not take delivery of the commodity. The markets tend to be more volatile than the share markets even though the theory suggests that speculators dealing on margin should help to smooth price movements. However, a study of the long-term charts of the daily price movements gives a clear impression of dangerous volatility. Speculation in this field is highly risky.

It is extremely difficult to construct models of individual commodities. Major international manufacturers have met with little success in predicting movements in individual commodity prices from models specifying supply and demand. Little has been gained from carrying out inspections of the growing crops and experience suggests that the combination of forces at work in the markets is virtually impossible to quantify within meaningful bounds of probability.

We therefore suggest that firms,which have to buy commodities on a regular basis to get the supplies which form the basis of their products, should not attempt to make elaborate price forecasts and should not 'play' the futures markets. Yet volatile material costs must be reckoned with in estimating the range of total cost movements and the implications for the pricing of the finished product. A surge in a key commodity price will force producers to raise the product price. All competitors in that market will react in the same way, but the total market for the product may shrink in response to the price increase if that increase is greater than the general rate of price inflation.

In food markets sharp price changes can lead to substitutions. A glut, depressing prices, may lead to increased consumption at the expense of another food product. Conversely, a shortage of potatoes, for example, may lead to increased consumption of rice and pasta. The same tendency can be observed in the meat markets where oversupply depresses the price of a meat product and results in a substitution of that item for other, more expensive, meat products.

Surpluses and shortages are difficult to forecast. In wine production the wine harvest can be spoiled by an early frost. Weather fluctuations of this kind are unpredictable. The forecaster is therefore compelled to take a long view of demand and supply for a commodity and to project a range within which the price is likely to fluctuate. It is then possible to present scenarios showing the cost effects of the higher and lower prices in the forecast range.

The importance of charts

The maintenance of up-to-date charts of the commodity price is indispensable. Commodity brokers, dealers and traders invariably study the entrails of a chart, its highs and lows, seasonality, trends and trading volumes. The price history has to be analysed in conjunction with an estimate in the trend from cycle to cycle in the demand for the commodity. That trend has to be related to spending power measured in real terms. Thus the demand for wheat will be related both to the changing size of the population and to the changing level of its purchasing power.

In richer countries rising purchasing power may be accompanied by a decline in consumption of wheat products, diets becoming more varied as family affluence increases. Wheat, however, has to be analysed as part of a world market made up of a host of societies at different stages of economic development, ranging from extreme poverty and malnutrition to the relative prosperity of the USA.

Every commodity must be analysed in the context of a world market. Demand for copper, for example, must be looked at in relation to the growth in industrial production. That relationship will reflect changes in technology tending to result in a lower demand for copper. Over a period of 50 years the volume of copper required at a certain level of industrial production has gradually declined. The copper price has also to be examined against the capacity of the world's copper mining industry, bearing in mind that capacity is inelastic in the short run since it takes several years to open up a new mine and to bring it into production.

Forecasting of a commodity price should therefore incorporate the following steps:

- Obtain or compile a chart of the price going back over the past 12 years or more. Financial data of this kind is increasingly available via the Internet.
- Join the peaks and join the troughs so as to illustrate the boundaries of the price fluctuations.
- Calculate and plot a 120-day moving average of the price series to help establish a trend.
- Measure the average price fluctuations and the extreme fluctuations as a percentage of the trend price.
- Calculate the long-term trend rate of change in the price. Compare this with world or OECD indicators for gross domestic product (GDP). Compare with industrial production for base metals and rubber. Use household or consumer spending for food and fibre products.

- Calculate the ratio between the commodity price rate of change and the rate of change in GDP and industrial production or consumer spending.
- Establish a forecast rate of change for world or OECD GDP, industrial production or consumer spending.
- Apply the historic ratio for the relationship with the commodity, as in (vi), to establish a forecast trend rate of change in the commodity price.
- Apply the historic average price fluctuations, as in (iv), to the predicted price trend to illustrate a probable range of price movements of the commodity. Also apply the extreme historic fluctuations to illustrate the boundaries of risk.
- Use the range of predictions to illustrate the possible changes in costs from the variations of the commodity price affecting the total cost of the finished product.

Conclusions

- The world's climate will become more volatile as a result of global warming.
- Effective measures to cut carbon emissions may take as long as 50 years to produce results. Sea levels will continue to rise while rising temperatures will have profound effects on wind and rain patterns and all forms of animal life and vegetation.
- The cost of insurance cover for climatic disasters will continue to rise, affecting both businesses and households.
- Agriculture and food production will be seriously affected as some regions become infertile whilst others become more productive. Many countries will be confronted by water shortage.
- Low-lying areas will face the risk of inundation and coastal erosion will increase. Development plans in those areas have to take account of the chances of damage and destruction over the life of any potential construction project.
- Apart from the long-term impact of climate change, some industries need short-term weather forecasts up to a week ahead to plan production and distribution.
- Energy investments have long life spans, requiring long-term forecasts taking into account legislation and tax changes as well as competing energy sources.
- Agricultural commodity prices are affected by climatic change. That apart, all commodity prices are highly volatile and the forecaster must use long-term charts to illustrate the volatility and risks.
- Elaborate forecasts of a commodity price are impractical. The forecaster should use charts of daily price movements covering 12 years or more to establish long-term trends, cyclical movements and the boundaries of fluctuation.
- These should be related to major economic trends to generate a trend and a risk forecast for a specific commodity price.

Sources

Climate and the Affairs of Men (Browning and Nels Winkless).
The Regional Impact of Climate Change (Intergovernmental Panel on Climate Change).

Review of the Potential Effects of Climate Change in the United Kingdom (Climate Change Impacts Review Group for the Department of the Environment).

The End of the World (Leslie).

Predicting the Future: the Darwin College Lectures.

The *Economist*, weekly.

'Main Economic Indicators', OECD, monthly.

For commodity price history and charts, apply to your commodity broker.

5 POPULATION, SOCIAL TRENDS AND LIFESTYLES

Population and social trends change gradually. Changes from year to year are scarcely perceptible and the majority of forecasts pay no regard to these factors. Yet over a period of years the gradual changes add up to something quite significant. The size and age structures of populations change, with important consequences for markets. Equally, social trends, influenced by changing age structures, materialism and political pressures, evolve over long phases. Social change is reflected in lifestyles which also respond to changes in spending power and technology. The forecaster must be aware of these subtle changes in constructing predictions of household spending and the consumer markets.

Population growth

Population growth began to accelerate in France and England in the 18th century. The improvement in food supply associated with the agricultural revolution in England contributed to some improvement in health and survival rates. Yet progress was uneven and Britain's population fell briefly in the mid-18th century as a result of excessive gin drinking.

Britain's population exploded during the 19th century and that experience provides us with a textbook example of population behaviour which was to follow from country to country through the 20th and into the 21st centuries. Britain's first population census was compiled in 1801 and was repeated at ten-year intervals. The population expansion recorded in the following 200 years has been in sharp contradiction to the theory advanced by Thomas Malthus in his famous 'Essay on the Principle of Population' published in 1798.

The population of Britain increased from 10·5 million in 1801 to 20·8 million in 1851 and to 37·0 million in 1901. The rate of increase through the century averaged 1·3 per cent per annum and, although this was exceptional for the 19th century, much higher growth rates have been recorded by many other countries in the 20th century.

But for emigration, however, Britain's 19th-century population explosion would have been far higher. The Industrial Revolution contributed to faster population growth. At the same time, the improvements in both inland and sea transport opened up the possibilities of movement. The harsh conditions and poor prospects in Britain and Europe made the option of moving to a new country, offering cheap or free land, a gamble worth taking. This was in spite of the huge risks of a dangerous sea voyage, and of disease and untold privations in the New World.

It was not the destitute and feeble but the stronger elements of society who took their chance by emigrating. The financial costs were substantial and the evidence suggests that the USA, Canada, South Africa, Australia and New Zealand gained from the inflow of a younger, stronger, more fertile and more enterprising sample of population from the Old World.

In the first half of the century, Britain's population increase was largely due to a rising birth rate. Infant mortality remained high and disease took a huge toll. As a result, average life expectancy remained low. Life expectancy is estimated to have averaged 40 years at birth in 1840 and no higher than 41 in 1870. In the intervening years the rapid increase in factory production and the expansion of industrial towns led to overcrowding and appalling housing conditions, with inadequate sanitation and water supplies. Public health hazards were extremely high and frequent cholera outbreaks and the spread of turberculosis contributed to the high death rates.

The reductions in mortality through the 20th century reflected the improvements in medicine and the curbing and eradication of a number of infectious diseases. The lessening of poverty also led to higher standards of nutrition, while the improvements in housing and reduction in overcrowding helped to reduce illness and disease and to extend the life span.

In the meantime, fertility, having risen to a peak at the end of the 19th century, has progressively declined. The rise in the birth rate in the second half of the 19th century was largely due to the improving child survival rate. The average number of pregnancies remained at a high level, but higher numbers of babies survived.

Population decline

Economic factors contributed to the reduction of family size through the 20th century. The higher the level of education and income of the woman, the greater the likelihood of her having a smaller family. This trend has continued and, with the advent of the contraceptive pill in the 1960s women now have virtually complete control of their own fertility. The net result has been a profound change in family size and family life, women now achieving far greater economic independence. From 1974, the fertility rate for the UK as a whole has been persistently below the replacement rate of 2·1 babies per female.

As illustrated in Table 5.1 and Diagram 5.1, Britain's population rose from 37 million in 1901 to nearly 49 million in 1951 and will probably level out at over 60 million before 2011.

Table 5.1   The population of Britain from 1801 (millions)

1801	10.5	**2001**	59.2
1851	20.8	**2051**	49–54
1901	37.0	**2101**	34–44
1951	48.8		

Thus the whole cycle from poverty and low life expectancy in Britain through population explosion to a population peak has taken 200 years. That cycle of rising fertility and falling mortality is the pattern we have since witnessed in all parts of the world. The cycle is likely to be less than 200 years for the current developing countries since the acceleration of technology and the spread of knowledge will lead to the fertility rate declining at a faster rate. Thus the population explosions are likely to be compressed into a shorter span in the 21st century.

Diagram 5.1   Britain's population explosion

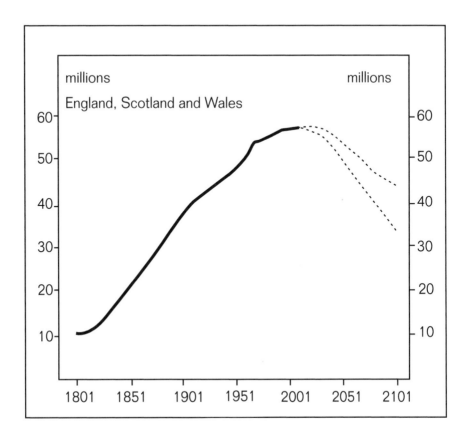

The decline in Britain's population growth through the 20th century stems from the fall in the fertility rate to below the replacement level from 1974 onwards. It seems highly unlikely that there will be a social and economic change sufficient to induce women to have more babies. Indeed, an increasing number of women remain childless.

That downward drift in the population level will be moderated by the trend towards higher life expectancy. Better health and advances in medicine tend to reduce the incidence of death at lower ages. This means that more people tend to survive into old age. The number of centenarians in the UK rose from 300 in 1951 to 4390 in 1991 and similar increases have been recorded in other advanced countries.

The population level will also be influenced by migration. The UK, along with other rich countries, has restricted and almost halted the intake of people from poor countries. Yet, as the decline in the population level gathers pace, attitudes may change and immigration into the UK may rise later in the 21st century. This would check the population fall.

For these reasons a wide band has to be set around the more distant population forecasts. It is quite possible that, at the end of the 21st century, Britain's population will have fallen back to the level it was at the beginning of the 20th century – 200 years previously. We conclude that, from a peak of over 59 million in 2001, Britain's population will decline to between 34 and 44 million through the course of the 21st century.

World population

Whilst the UK may provide a useful model to help predict the speed and size of population growth in developing countries, the growth rate of the world's population as a whole reflects the low birth rates of the mature developed countries.

The United Nations collects data and estimates of population country by country and publishes regular projections of world population levels. The UN's work in this field includes detailed studies of fertility rates and mortality, including estimates of the effects of the AIDS epidemic.

The rate of growth of the world's population has been slackening since around 1970, and to a greater extent in the 1990s than had been predicted. This change has been brought about by a greater decline in world fertility. As a result, population growth at the end of the 20th century had decelerated to under 1·5 per cent per annum, compared with 2 per cent in the early 1960s. The rate of growth and total population levels from 1950 are shown in Table 5.2 for the average of five-year periods. The table also shows the UN central projection out to 2045.

The projections show population growth in the more developed regions coming to an end in 2030 and a decline in population from that point onwards. Population is already declining in some European countries. In the less developed regions the rate of population growth appears to have peaked in the 1970s. The projected fall in population growth in those regions suggests that the growth rate will have declined to under 0·7 per cent per annum by around 2040. This also suggests that population change in the developing regions is lagging the more developed regions by 60–70 years.

Table 5.2 World population growth to 2045: United Nations' projection

	Annual rate of population change % increase			World population (billions)
	World total	More developed regions	Less developed regions	At end of period
1950–55	1.78	1.20	2.05	2.75
1960–65	1.99	1.10	2.36	3.34
1970–75	1.96	0.81	2.37	4.08
1980–85	1.73	0.56	2.09	4.85
1990–95	1.57	0.40	1.88	5.72
2000–05	1.37	0.25	1.63	6.59
2010–15	1.20	0.18	1.41	7.47
2020–25	1.00	0.10	1.17	8.29
2030–35	0.78	–0.08	0.92	9.01
2040–45	0.57	–0.14	0.67	9.59

Looking further ahead, the trends point to a levelling off of the world's population somewhere around 2080 at under 11 billion. Thus on those assumptions the total population seems likely to increase by some 4 billion during the course of the 21st century, a rise of 75 per cent from the level of the year 2001. Yet that projected increase, if correct, compares with a very much faster rate of increase through the 20th century and a rise in total population of about the same number.

Lower fertility

Changes in fertility have the largest impact on future population levels. According to the UN's figures the world fertility rate declined by 13 per cent in the decade 1980–85 to 1990–95. The decline was greater in the countries of East and South East Asia, particularly in China, as well as in Central and South America and Northern Africa.

The most important factor contributing to these declines is the increase in the use of contraceptives. In the developing countries this is largely a result of population and health policies as well as the increasing education of women. In some countries marriages have been taking place at a later age and this, too, has helped reduce fertility rates.

Education of women throughout the world has played a vital role in reducing fertility rates. In the 1990s almost twice as many women as men were illiterate. Illiterate girls tend to marry young and have a large number of children. Research work by the World Bank suggests that, where women are excluded from secondary education, the average woman has seven children. Thus high fertility is not related exclusively to illiteracy but is more likely to be determined by the extent of a woman's education.

Educated women have fewer babies and this, in turn, reveals the link between a woman's employment opportunities and her ability to earn an income. The demand for economic security is extremely strong and with the widespread breakdown of marriage in western society there is an added incentive for the woman to achieve a high degree of financial independence. The absolute dependence of the woman on the man in terms of spending power has been, and still is, extremely widespread in most societies. The woman is degraded; thus, with the attainment of higher levels of education, she will seize the opportunity to take paid employment to secure some degree of financial independence and will choose to limit her fertility.

Educated women have healthier babies and are better mothers. The increasing access of women to secondary and higher education has been the main highway towards smaller families. A greater understanding of contraception has resulted in substantial falls in fertility rates and the downward trend will continue. Indeed, it is difficult to know where it will stop. In spite of the opposition of the Roman Catholic Church to contraception, the fertility rate in both Italy and Spain has fallen further than in Protestant Europe, to no more than 1·2 per female (see Diagram 5.2).

We live in a highly materialistic world and almost universal access to television has created a growing appetite for more affluent lifestyles and more possessions. This in itself is likely to accelerate the pressure for greater female equality, for access to education and paid employment. There must therefore be fairly strong odds on the fertility rate in developing countries falling at a faster rate.

In this connection it is constructive to look at those countries which have advanced from a depressed to a developed economic status in the period

Diagram 5.2 European fertility

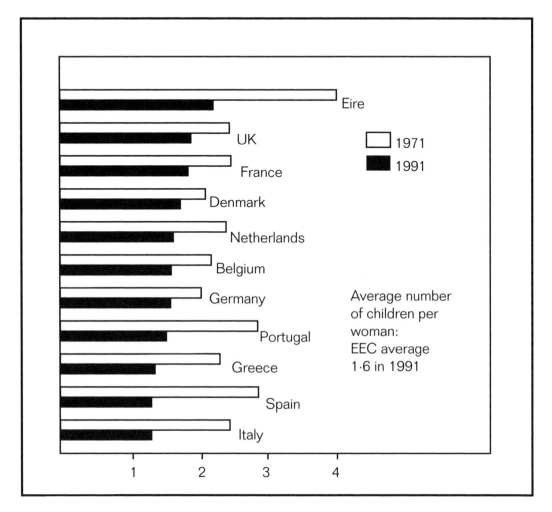

from 1950. South Korea, Hong Kong and Singapore have fertility rates of under two, whilst Thailand, China, Indonesia, the Philippines and Malaysia are all within sight of fertility rates down to the replacement level. Even in India the fertility rate is already at or below the replacement level in the three states of Goa, Kerala and Tamil Nadu.

These individual changes are reflected in the regional summary compiled by the UN, and Table 5.3 contrasts the fertility rates for the more and less developed regions as well as for Eastern Europe. The estimates show the averages for five-year periods. There was an acceleration in the rate of decline in fertility between the early 1980s and the early 1990s. This was particularly so in the case of the more developed regions and Eastern Europe.

Table 5.3   Changes in fertility rates

| | Total fertility rate: births per woman | | Change in total fertility rate (%) | |
| | | | 1980–85 to 1985–90 | 1985–90 to 1990–95 |
	1980–85	1990–95		
More developed regions	1.84	1.70	–0.5	–7.1
Less developed regions	4.15	3.48	–7.7	–9.1
Eastern Europe	2.06	1.62	1.5	–22.5
WORLD TOTAL	3.58	3.10	–5.6	–8.3

In the case of Eastern Europe, the economic disruptions following the collapse of the communist regimes in 1990 were acute and protracted. Economic hardship must have had an effect on fertility in parallel with the fall in fertility in the 1930s slump. One reason for a decline in fertility in 'hard times' is the likelihood of marriages being deferred. Later marriages reduce the chances of pregnancy.

The evidence suggests that the decline in fertility is becoming more broad-based and sustained in Saharan Africa, and South and West Asia, whilst the transition to fertility decline became apparent in sub-Saharan Africa in the early 1990s. In West and South Asia fertility decline is continuing in India and accelerating in Bangladesh. The Islamic religion favours large families but the overall trend is equally towards lower fertility through most of the Islamic world.

The world trend suggests there must be good odds on the overall fertility rate falling to the replacement level at some point in the 2020s. If that proves correct then world population may level out in the 2050s, earlier than predicted.

Mortality

Life expectancy continues to rise, offsetting to some extent the effects on population levels of falling fertility. Life expectancy for the world as a whole averaged nearly 65 years in the early 1990s while Japan has the world's highest life expectancy at birth, averaging 77 for men and 83 for women.

The USA, with an end of 20th century population of around 270 million, is estimated to have close to 100 000 centenarians. Given the right combination of health and wealth, life expectancy will continue to increase and research into the ageing process will generate knowledge, helping to extend the *average* life span towards 100 and beyond.

The extension of life expectancy on this scale will be feasible in the mature economies with high average levels of income. The elimination of childhood illnesses will make a large contribution to increasing life spans, whilst health education will help people to avoid the diseases of affluence arising from smoking, excessive liquor and fat consumption, stress and obesity. More and more people are now taking regular exercise. The membership of health clubs is on a rising trend and there is a growing awareness of the importance to health of a balanced diet. These trends will continue, helping to reduce mortality rates.

At the other extreme, poverty remains the world's biggest killer, particularly of children. The World Health Organization estimates that one-fifth of the world's population lives in extreme poverty and that almost one-third of the world's children are undernourished. Poverty-linked diseases such as cholera, tuberculosis and plague have been rising in rich as well as poor countries, while immunization against fatal childhood diseases is dropping. As a result life expectancy has been *falling* towards an average of 40 years at birth in the poorest countries, such as the Ivory Coast, the Central African Republic, Congo, Uganda and Zambia. Yet in mid-19th century Britain, in the course of industrialization, life expectancy stayed around 40 in spite of substantial economic advances, and the major reduction in mortality was only achieved following major spending on water and sewage schemes and other public health measures. A similar transition is likely in the world's poorest countries in the first half of the 21st century.

However, the inequalities of income within countries, rich and poor alike, are likely to continue. This implies that the poverty-linked diseases will continue to take their toll. Moreover, the AIDS epidemic is spreading and the death toll is rising rapidly. The incidence of sexually transmitted diseases has been rising and that trend also seems likely to continue. A cumulative total of over 20 million people have been infected with HIV since the late 1970s and the number of HIV-positive people was estimated to be 40 million at the end of the 20th century.

The UN's population estimates draw out the impact of AIDS; in the 15 hardest hit countries, the toll from AIDS has reduced life expectancy at birth by three years. This feature will reduce the population growth rate in those countries. The UN short-term projection is shown in Table 5.4.

The UN estimates illustrate the growing impact of AIDS on population levels. For the 15 sub-Saharan countries, AIDS is reducing population growth, so that by 2005 the total population will be nearly 4 per cent lower than it would have been without the epidemic. For the three countries Uganda, Zambia and Zimbabwe, the impact on the total population will be a

Table 5.4 Population size with and without AIDS for sub-Saharan countries (millions)

	1990	*1995*	*2000*	*2005*
15 sub-Saharan countries				
with AIDS	189.4	221.2	254.6	291.8
without AIDS	189.8	223.4	260.8	303.4
difference (%)	–0.2	–1.0	–2.4	–3.8
Uganda, Zambia & Zimbabwe				
with AIDS	36.0	42.0	47.9	54.2
without AIDS	36.1	42.8	49.9	57.9
difference (%)	–0.3	–1.7	–4.1	–6.5

reduction of over 6 per cent by 2005. In the absence of an effective cure, population growth will continue to decelerate, not least because younger people are the prime casualties of the disease. Fertility will therefore be reduced, making further inroads into population growth.

The AIDS epidemic illustrates the vulnerability of mankind to disease where there is little or no natural resistance and no known antidote. The possibility must be recognized that, as a result of global warming, the incidence of dangerous diseases may increase. The malaria-carrying mosquito, for example, is likely to find favourable habitats in areas of the world which are currently free from malaria. There are unpredictable possibilities of virulent strains of disease emerging to afflict many animal species, including man.

The balance of probability suggests that, for all man's inventiveness and ingenuity, not enough will be done to halt global warming, so that in the second half of the 21st century population levels will be affected by the greater incidence of infectious diseases. Those outbreaks may be of such a scale that severe population losses will occur before antidotes have been discovered and brought into general use.

Thus the trend towards greater longevity in the richer segments of world society may ultimately be offset by the greater incidence of disease. It may well be, therefore, that world mortality rates will not decline to the same degree as through the 20th century and as a result world population growth will come to a halt at an earlier date and at a lower total than widely expected.

Immigration

The transition to far longer life spans is likely to be slow and lengthy. In the meantime the ageing of society in the developed countries, where the population levels have already flattened out or begun to fall, will produce a growing imbalance. The proportion of older people, above conventional working age, will go on expanding. There will eventually be a shortage of younger people to produce the services and generate the wealth to pay a growing volume of pensions. The population of such a society will be declining, since the chances are that more and more women will have chosen to have full-time paid employment. More and more will be childless and the fertility rate will edge still lower.

As this scenario unfolds attitudes towards immigration may change. Governments may ultimately welcome an influx of young migrants from the less-developed countries so as to restore a more acceptable population age structure. Though this seems highly unlikely at the turn of the century, within 20 or 30 years Western Europe may begin to open its frontiers to a steady intake of young people from the overpopulated and poor developing regions.

Migration has expanded sharply in Europe since the 1990 revolutions. As the ex-communist countries lifted the barriers to movement, emigration increased substantially, mostly towards Western Europe. On the other side of the world, immigration continues at a significant level into the USA, in spite of the legal obstacles to entry. Illegal entry from the south is substantial and population growth in the USA is sustained by the net inflow.

Global warming will lead to increasing pressures for population movement. The gradual increase in sea levels and the growing incidence of storms and cyclones will result in more widespread flooding and loss of fertile land. In densely populated countries such as Bangladesh, more and more people will be forced to move and, with a scarcity of land and resources in their home countries, the pressures to emigrate will expand.

The problem will be acute in China and India, and governments may be unable to prevent large-scale movements of people across frontiers. These will be the seeds of international conflict and, looking ahead to the end of the 21st century, there will by then have been a large redistribution of parts of the world's population.

Forecasting the population

The UN estimates and forecasts of population will suffice for most business purposes. The advanced countries produce their own estimates and projections. Where longer-term forecasts are required, the forecaster may wish to construct independent forecasts.

The track record of official population forecasts is not impressive. The evidence suggests that government agencies are cautious and slow to recognize social change. Fertility rates rose in the prosperous period following the Second World War. Population forecasts, however, assumed that birth rates would drop back to the depressed levels of the 1930s.

Fertility rates began to fall in the 1960s in the USA and then in Europe. Yet official projections still assumed continued high birth rates. In addition, the increase in life expectancy has been underestimated in official projections and it is for these reasons that businesses should check the population projections for the markets in which they operate.

Changing population age structures are of particular importance over the longer term since the age segments of the population to which firms sell may well expand or contract to a greater extent than suggested by the official projections.

Migration is the likeliest source of error in population forecasts. Whereas births and deaths in the great majority of countries have to be registered by law, estimates of migration are based on samples of arrivals and departures at airports, seaports and border posts. There is also a significant element of illegal immigration, notably in the USA, so that a more accurate picture of migration only emerges after the periodic census of population. The census will generally produce a different population total from that derived from the annual estimates of births, deaths and migration. Censuses are held in most countries at ten-year intervals and the discrepancies in estimates that then emerge are largely due to mistaken migration estimates.

Social change

Social change was pronounced through the 20th century. There has been a major change in the position of women, a vast improvement in health and working conditions, a great increase in average living standards and a great extension of education and literacy.

Taking the world as a whole, the improvements achieved in the richest societies in the 20th century will extend through the poorer societies in the 21st century. 'Keeping up with the Joneses' is one of the safest laws of forecasting. What the top income groups do today is an indicator of how the middle income groups will spend their money in a generation's time. We live in a highly materialistic world where envy is a great motivator. People want more things: better houses, bigger cars, longer holidays and so on.

Television has been the vehicle for the spread of materialism over the past 50 years. It illustrates how other people live. Films show different lifestyles so that the humblest and poorest viewer is made aware of the range of things available, given sufficient purchasing power. The growth of materialism is not solely a product of modern advertising but is derived from the wide range of television programmes. Much of the material originates from the USA. Thus the world's richest society is a role model for people in many developing countries. The law of 'keeping up with the Joness' tells us that spending patterns and lifestyles through the 21st century will move towards the standards achieved by the USA at the end of the 20th century.

The pace of social change has accelerated with the advances in technology, education and literacy. This is apparent from the time taken to establish personal freedoms, human rights and equality before the law. The struggle to establish religious toleration in Western Europe has been a long and protracted story from the 16th century onwards. Discrimination against non-conformists led to the first waves of migration, principally from England to North America, in the 17th century. Although freedom of religion became a tenet of the American states, Catholics and non-conformists faced penal laws and discrimination up to the 19th century.

Although firmly entrenched in most western democracies, freedom of religion is still not universally observed even though laid down in constitutional law. Religious bigotry and intolerance runs deep in some countries, as is vividly illustrated in Northern Ireland, Israel and some Muslim countries. Tolerance has increased with the spread of education. Even so, militant minorities exert a powerful influence and these ideological differences will continue.

The abolition of slavery has been a long and painful progress. In spite of growing public concern among church congregations during the 18th century, it took decades of political pressure to secure the international outlawing of the slave trade in 1815. Slavery in the USA was only abolished with the defeat of the Confederate States in the Civil War in the 1860s. Slavery has still not been completely eradicated and, in desperately poor societies, children as well as adults are bought and sold for their labour.

As with religion, the establishment of personal freedom, freedom of the press and the right to liberty has taken many years and the process is by no means complete. Change in these instances does not appear to have accelerated. In the case of female emancipation and equality between the sexes, progress has been more rapid. As in most movements, the USA has tended to lead the way. In Britain, women did not obtain the right to vote until 1918. This was restricted to ladies over the age of 30, the voting age being reduced to 21 in 1928.

Female equality

Electoral reform was only the beginning in the trend towards female equality and the ending of discrimination between the sexes. Most males have had little understanding of the vulnerability of women in society and the legal bondage imposed by marriage laws. More importantly the woman, in most marriages, has been utterly dependent in economic terms on her husband. The demands of pregnancy and child rearing reduce a wife in many cases to a condition of virtual slavery. With no income of her own, the dependence upon the man has been complete and it is only since the First World War that women in the western world have begun to achieve some degree of economic independence through being able to take paid employment other than domestic service.

The attempt to achieve economic independence is logical in two respects. First, women have suffered the indignity of having to depend on the husband – the breadwinner – to hand over money every pay day to keep house in the following week. The dependence upon the male has been overwhelming and the male's behaviour has often been brutal and capricious. Secondly, marriages have become more impermanent. Divorce rates have risen to high proportions so that in the USA the expectancy is that the marriage partnership will be dissolved sooner or later.

The likelihood of divorce increases the need for the woman to achieve and increase her economic independence. The consequence has been that women have campaigned for equal opportunities within the employment market. They have also limited the incidence of child bearing so as to be able to return to the world of paid employment. In a growing number of cases, women choose to remain childless in order to pursue a career.

There has therefore been an overwhelming economic motive for women to demand equal employment opportunities. Social change in this field has been rapid and discrimination on grounds of gender has been outlawed in the mature democracies – as it was in the communist dictatorships. Yet equality between the sexes is far from complete and further change will be made in this direction through the century. The most obvious bar to equality is in pregnancy and child raising. The interruption of a working career by pregnancy is not shared by the man, except to a minor extent where the father is able to take paternity leave under social security provisions.

Absolute equality in terms of a career, work opportunity and financial reward is unattainable except in limited fields, such as the arts. Nevertheless, the drive towards female equality will be maintained. In the advanced economies women are now equalling, or surpassing, men in most levels of education. In 2001 and 2002 young women seem set to be better educated and qualified than their male counterparts. This, coupled with the drive for economic independence and a determination to make a career outside the home, will perpetuate the low levels of female fertility.

Age discrimination

Interest in the problem of discrimination in employment on grounds of age was a feature of the last years of the 20th century. As with other progressive movements, the USA is again leading the way and a vigorous campaign is being waged by older people to end discrimination and to establish equality of opportunity. There is a powerful economic motive behind the movement, since many people of conventional retirement age need additional income to supplement their pension entitlements.

This age group accounts for a growing proportion of the population and its size and importance will increase. It therefore has a significant political clout and legislation is already in place to allow older people to retain their jobs, should the work still be available. Many older people still have commitments to families. Late marriages, often following divorce, may result in children being in higher education at the point where the parents reach retirement age. An American social feature is the large number of small businesses owned and run by older people, often providing services to the elderly community.

The mature western societies are likely to follow the American pattern and legislation will be enacted in the 21st century aimed at outlawing discrimination on the grounds of age. Confronted by the relative shortage of young people, social security systems will be amended to encourage older people to defer retirement. By mid-century, the pattern of employment will have changed significantly, work being shared more evenly through the age groups.

The problems associated with an ageing population are likely to become more acute later in the century. With the advances in medicine, more people will survive into old age. Indeed, with the introduction of genetic engineering, death is likely to be deferred into a longer old age.

Genetic engineering

The cloning of the sheep, Dolly, in Britain in 1997 has focused attention on the enormous range of possibilities opened up by genetic engineering. In plant technology genetic engineering has already been applied in modifying species widely used in the food chain. European countries have banned the import of some genetically engineered food products from the USA and the ethics of the science is hotly disputed.

We are on the brink of a scientific revolution of dramatic proportions. Genetic engineering will be applied without question to the whole range of disease. The increasing intensity of research, accelerated by the communications revolution, promises to reveal the means of eradicating cancer, for example. It will unlock the causes of Alzheimer's disease and dementia and help reduce one of the great tragedies of ageing. Thus the possibilities arising from the products of the biotechnological industry are infinite. Apart from the gradual conquest and reduction in the incidence of disease, man will be capable of lengthening the average human life span.

This trend is already apparent in the increasing number of centenarians. In the USA the number of centenarians is projected to rise to around 1·2 million by 2050, compared with some 100 000 at the end of the 20th century. The OECD has estimated that the proportion of the population over 80 in the mature economies will rise to around 6 per cent by 2040, compared with just over 3 per cent in 1990. Taking the effect of falling fertility rates into account, together with the increase in life expectancy, the share of the population over 80 will rise even more sharply by the year 2100, towards 15 per cent. By the end of the century the elderly population will therefore account for a proportion of more than four times its share in the year 2000.

The increase in longevity is impressive, and this is without a contribution to the trend from genetic engineering. Allowing for a long time lag before the results of research are translated into the production of genetic cures for cancer and other diseases, the trend towards longer life spans will strengthen. The impact of the revolution in biochemistry will be modest initially, since development may be hampered by legal restraints and costs. Yet man's natural instinct to cling to life and to prolong his life span suggests that many individuals will spend large sums on the new treatments.

The likelihood is that in the rich, mature countries life expectancy at birth will rise to as much as 100 by the end of the 21st century. The age structure of the population in those countries will be transformed, and with complex social consequences. One risk of greater longevity is that minds may deteriorate faster than bodies. In any event the last stages of life tend to be accompanied by illness and the requirement for medical attention and care will still be substantial, regardless of the contributions from genetic engineering.

The rise in life expectancy will partially offset the decline in birth rates. As a result, the fall in the total level of population will be gradual rather than sudden. Even so, the ageing of the population may generate concern at the relative shortage of children and young people. This is unlikely to be met by large-scale immigration. It may lead to the payment of substantial subsidies to women to increase the birth rate. It may also lead to the acceptance of the manipulation of human genetic reproduction.

The decline of the family

Although these developments in biochemistry will have profound social consequences, it should not be supposed that man's fundamental human nature will be changed. We are as Darwin described us, products of a continuous process of evolution, programmed to survive and cling to life as part of the survival of the fittest. We are inherently selfish and self-centred, like any other animal species. Our natural lifestyle is to form families, for families to live in villages and to form tribes.

Changes in social patterns are slow and, for all the acceleration in technological development and communications, many aspects of our lives are unchanging. We eat, reproduce, work, play and sleep and the changes in technology take place around these stable, recurring features of human life. The ageing of society, smallness of families and incidence of childless people living alone will have a profound effect on the character of society, in which we are all interdependent. The family unit will be less of a force for caring for its members and there will be a growing need for caring services provided by the state or other organizations.

Since we are predominantly social animals the likelihood is that individuals will participate to a greater extent in club-like groups and activities. Holidays, for example, are organized to meet that kind of need and the growing popularity of cruises illustrates that trend. Special-interest holidays and holidays for 'singles' are part of an expanding social market.

There has been a marked decline in religious belief. In the 19th century, religion and the family were the cement of society. With the increase in technology, the advance of science, the spread of literacy and knowledge and the rise in living standards, the acceptance of religious discipline has weakened. This has contributed to a loosening of family ties and obligations. In the past, sexual promiscuity was likely to result in illegitimate births. Bastardy led to shame and social ostracism. Women were therefore subject to the kind of social restraints which can still be found today in some Catholic countries.

Medical science has largely removed the link between sexual promiscuity and illegitimacy by the invention of near-foolproof methods of birth control. This has resulted in greater sexual experiment and freedom and has contributed to the rising incidence of family breakdown and divorce. Yet the clock is unlikely to be turned back.

In addition, the ease of travel has led to a great increase in mobility. Whereas in the past the majority of the people lived and worked in close communities, a greater proportion now travel to work. The increase in mobility has made it easier for people to move to other areas to work and this has also contributed to the weakening of family ties. Moreover, the increasing difficulty in finding work will sustain the pressures on families in the first part of the 21st century, perpetuating low birth rates and separating families over longer distances.

Future lifestyles

In a highly materialistic society the continuous advances in technology generate new products and new appetites. A striking feature of the 20th century was the reduction of household drudgery. The demands of cooking, cleaning and washing absorbed much of the housewife's working day in a round of tiring manual labour. Labour-saving devices and new products have reduced household drudgery. The trend will continue and the fact that a majority of women go out to work adds to the pressures to reduce housework. In recent years the microwave oven and pre-prepared meals have made a major contribution to reducing the time spent in the kitchen.

The trend towards reduction in housework will continue, increasing the margin of leisure time. This is also reflected in the rising number of meals eaten out. Eating out will continue to expand, to the point where a third to half of all meals in the mature societies will be eaten outside the home.

Increasing affluence and the shortening of the working year will generate strong growth in spending on holidays. Many families already take more than one annual holiday, plus a number of weekend breaks. Distances travelled have lengthened dramatically with the reduction in the costs of air travel and it is not uncommon for people to travel many thousands of miles on holiday. A more rational sharing of work will maintain the trend towards more holiday travel.

As living standards rise in the developing countries, still more people will join the army of tourists. Congestion of airspace, airports and the roads serving them will increase to the point where the discomforts of travel lead to changes in tourism. The airship may eventually come into its own, offering greater comfort to the passenger at a more sedate pace. One possibility is that man will imitate the birds, migrating for part of the year, to avoid the worst of the winter weather, to holiday homes in the less crowded parts of the globe, such as Australia and Africa.

Leisure activity in the home area will expand. There will be greater participation in sports and increasing membership of health and fitness clubs. The concern to maintain and improve health and to combat obesity will lead to a more positive attitude to diet and exercise, and spending on health in its wider sense will account for a larger share of income. There is growing interest in alternative medicine and there is likely to be a substantial increase in self- medication, lessening the dependency on costly conventional medicine and public health services.

The advances in technology, coupled with the ageing of population in the mature countries, will contribute to changes in building and architecture. Housing conditions have improved dramatically from century to century. Overcrowding, common in the 18th and 19th centuries, has been progressively reduced and that trend will continue through the 21st century.

Population census returns show a steady reduction in the average number of occupants per house. In the 20th century the amount of floor space per person continued to rise. Room size in new housing has tended to increase and extra amenities, such as bathrooms, shower rooms, studies, utilities, spare bedrooms, garages and conservatories have become common features of wealthier societies.

The law of 'keeping up with the Joneses' points to the continued growth in household space and amenities in line with the long-term expansion of household spending power. At the beginning of the 20th century, many houses were still lit by candle or oil lamp. Gas lighting was available in towns and cities and a minority of houses were lit by electricity. Heating was generally provided by coal fires or stoves and most houses were draughty, cold and uncomfortable. The improvement in household comfort during the century was impressive. The great majority of property is now supplied with piped water, sanitation and central heating. Refrigeration has improved food hygiene and many houses are equipped with sophisticated cooking systems and dishwashers. The electronic and electrical revolutions have contributed to the massive growth of the telephone networks, to radio, television, the personal computer, the microwave oven and sophisticated security systems.

This catalogue of a century's technical progress in contributing to a family's physical comfort and enjoyment is impressive. There should be little doubt that invention and technical innovation will continue and that the ownership of this range of products and amenities will spread through populations across the world. We cannot predict the new discoveries which will become successful domestic products through the 21st century, but there will be further reductions in household drudgery. The home environment will be electronically controlled, as will home security.

New, or improved, materials will feature in building, enhancing heat conservation and reducing energy consumption and pollution. Climate change, generating greater extremes in rainfall, temperature and storm damage, will focus attention on building design and location. The costs of maintaining older housing will rise and the advantages offered by new technology and improved housing design will tend to lead to faster rates of house replacement in the mature economies.

This will be against a background of slowly falling population and an average household size declining to two persons or lower, tending to keep the total number of households at a stable level. There will be a growing demand for smaller housing units in terms of the number of rooms, but offering more space per person. At the same time the growth in second home ownership is likely to continue, depending upon the opportunities or limitations created by the transport networks. At some point, in some regions, traffic congestion may make travel so uncomfortable that personal mobility may decline, having a bearing on household location and lifestyle.

The increase in violence and crime will strengthen the demand for more effective home security and there will be widespread use of electronic systems of remote control, monitoring not only security but temperature, heating, lighting and kitchen appliances – in effect creating the intelligent home. Although drug-related crime may lessen later in the century, contributing to lower levels of housebreaking, electronic surveillance and control is likely to be maintained, becoming a standard feature of more and more property.

The private car

Personal transport is a great luxury and owning what amounts to a private carriage extends personal freedom. It is a remarkable fact that the plain man's motor car gives him far more mobility and comfort than was available to monarchs up to the late 19th century. It is hardly surprising, therefore, that car ownership exploded during the 20th century.

Multi-car ownership is now common in the mature economies, many households having two vehicles and some even more. In many cities and densely populated areas, car usage has become so intense that traffic congestion now causes long delays and long journey times. In those cases it contributes to the build-up of air pollution and the increase in asthma and lung infection. The increase in carbon emissions across the world has wider consequences in terms of the greenhouse effect. The stage has now been reached where the personal freedom conferred by car ownership impinges upon, and lessens, the freedom of society as a whole.

The conflict of interests resulting from car usage is likely to result in a long-drawn-out tug of war between car owners and the car industries on one side and the wider interests of mankind as a whole. Pollution has been targeted in some American states aimed at the speedy introduction of zero emission vehicles. Manufacturers, however, have not so far succeeded in producing electric-powered cars at an economic price. Research has intensified and there is substantial competition to get an electric vehicle powered by fuel cells into mass production.

Pollution will be curbed and reduced by a combination of improved fuel efficiency in the conventional petrol engine and the growth in market share of the electric car. These developments will not eliminate congestion. Neither will they reduce the demand for car ownership. Given the economic and demographic growth of the developing countries, car ownership will expand substantially through the 21st century. Car design and technology will continue to improve, incorporating new electronic control systems. Programmed routing of car journeys will make it possible to maintain traffic flow on major roads at greater densities, whilst small electric runabouts will replace conventional cars within towns and cities.

Thus the luxury of private car ownership will be sustained, albeit with less freedom for the motorist. The powerful habit of private motoring will provide a major stimulus for research and redevelopment of the motor vehicle so as to modify its anti-social tendencies.

Forecasting social change and lifestyles

Social changes help generate changes in lifestyles. For forecasting purposes, the USA provides a leading indicator for changes to come in other countries. The lifestyles of the rich set targets for other sections of the community and over a generation these styles filter downwards as the spending power of society rises.

It is possible, therefore, to predict changes not only by studying the patterns of spending and consumption in the USA but by examining those patterns of spending by the richer income groups within a country. International comparisons are not always reliable, however, since climatic differences are reflected in lifestyles.

There are other differences arising from population densities and the price of land. Much of the USA is favoured by generous land availability and modest land prices. This makes it possible to enjoy more spacious living conditions with larger houses and larger rooms, bigger roads and bigger cars. In Japan, and parts of Europe, land is scarce and prices are far higher. This results in greater building densities and smaller apartments.

The USA has led the way in a number of major social changes. Religious toleration, democratic government and the drive towards female equality and age equality are examples of American trail-blazing. The USA lagged, however, over the abolition of slavery and racial equality. Moreover, other countries pioneered developments in social security and provision of health services. The lesson for the forecaster is to maintain a constant watch on social and lifestyle changes around the world, recognizing that, with the speeding up of communications and travel, communities are more open to influences from other societies than ever before.

The increases in spending power, combined with the changes in age structures, will lead to the fragmentation of markets. The forecaster must recognize that the range of choice available to the consumer will widen. These options mean that the individual firm must look beyond its immediate market to allow for the impact of competition for the customer's spending power.

Conclusions

- Population growth declines with the rise in living standards and the increase in literacy and education. The trend towards female equality leads to a reduction in family size.
- The demand for economic security, and for a woman to have command of income of her own, contributes to later marriage, a growing degree of childlessness and a fall in fertility rates to below the replacement level.
- Life expectancy will continue to rise, helped by developments in genetic engineering.
- Population growth will be checked to some extent by AIDS and other infectious diseases where there is no known antidote.
- The ageing of society in the developed countries will produce a relative shortage of young people, which may result in increased immigration from less developed countries.
- The improvement achieved in the richer countries in the 20th century will extend through the poorer countries in the 21st century, being reflected in spending patterns and lifestyles.
- Further advances will be made towards female equality and discrimination on the grounds of age is likely to be outlawed.
- The family unit will be less of a force for caring for its members. There will be a growing need for caring services.

Sources

The Limits to Growth (Meadows *et al.*).

Beyond the Limits (Meadows *et al.*)

The End of the World (John Leslie).

The Regional Impact of Climate Change (Intergovernmental Panel on Climate Change).

Preparing for the Twenty First Century (Kennedy).

Remaking Eden (Silver).

Brave New World (Huxley).

World Economic and Social Survey (United Nations).

'The Capitalist Threat' (Soros).

6 TECHNICAL CHANGE, COMMUNICATIONS AND EDUCATION

We have only to list the major changes in technology achieved during the 20th century to recognize that industrial progress, stemming from the 18th century, is part of a continuous – and accelerating – industrial revolution. The internal combustion engine, the car, the aeroplane, the telephone, radio, television, plastics, antibiotics, nuclear energy, the computer – all have made a major impact on production and everyday life. The sum of man's technical achievements in that century is clearly far greater than the progress made in previous centuries.

The pace of change has accelerated through the last 500 years. The amount of time and resources devoted to learning has gone on rising and the improving means of communication have all contributed to speeding up the pace of change. Throughout time, increasing contact between peoples has contributed to the spread of knowledge, and the explosion of sea travel since the 15th century has increased trade and contact between different societies.

Our own knowledge of changes in production is exact so far as recent centuries are concerned. Our understanding of the scale and nature of change is far less precise. The technical landmarks, such as the printing press, the rotation of crops, the steam engine, the factory system, the great navigations, vaccination and so on, are well documented. They can be seen to be part of an accelerating wave of change that dwarfs the speed of technical innovation achieved by the countless ancestor generations which went before.

What is not so sure is why change happened at any particular instant. The exploitation of an invention is only made possible by applying an investment of other people's labour. The society in question has to be able to create a surplus – savings – which can release some of its members from the essential tasks of feeding the community and ensuring its survival.

Continuous industrial revolution

The pace of industrial change has been dictated by the creation of surplus in the form of savings. Those savings have financed investment and the rising level of investment has generated faster growth in output.

An invention is of little use without the resources to bring it into production. Man is remarkably inventive, but the effort of invention is less dependent on capital than on knowledge. In broad terms, it is the expanding flow of savings and investment which has led to the exploitation of invention and the resultant improvement in productivity, wealth and living standards.

Industrial change in the western world has moved in phases from the first Industrial Revolution, based on steam power, iron and steel. Towards the end of the 19th century, electricity, the internal combustion engine and major advances in chemistry laid the foundations of a second industrial revolution.

The continuous development of the electrical and chemical industries in the latter part of the 20th century led into a third major phase of industrial revolution. Electronics, with its myriad applications, has spawned new products and new industries. The speed of development, innovation and introduction of new products, such as the microwave oven and personal computer, has been unprecedented.

At the same time, laboratory research has opened up a new field of industrial application in the field of biotechnology. Because of the long test times required to prove new techniques, the revolutionary impact of biotechnology has been less obvious than that of electronics. Yet the industry's potential is just as far-reaching, and genetic engineering, however contentious the ethical questions raised, will undoubtedly make a powerful impact on industrial and agricultural development and on human affairs through the 21st century.

What we now call the communications revolution is also part of the third major wave of industrial change. Its features lie for the most part in the field of electronics. The breakthrough in computer technology came with the advance from the vacuum valve, first to the transistor and then to 'solid-logic' circuits and the microchip. As a result the computer was transformed from a gargantuan piece of equipment to a compact unit capable of operating at amazing speed.

The computer has transformed the printing industry. The newspaper industry was able to abandon the ancient, costly lead letter technology, displacing a large part of the labour force. The word processor, in conjunction with the photocopier, has speeded up printing and slashed its costs. Equally, fax has speeded up communications and enlarged the scope for transmitting messages.

Married to the telephone network, the computer has opened the way to almost instant access to information from a huge variety of sources. The development of fibre optics has at a leap transformed the potential capacity of the telephone system. Optical fibres are almost completely immune from interference and have a high resistance to heat. They are only a fraction of the weight of the standard cable. Fibre optic circuits allow a signal to be carried along strands of glass the thickness of a human hair. Each of those fibres is capable of carrying thousands of telephone calls. Thus fibre optics are displacing copper in the telephone networks, reducing the costs of communication and raising the capacity of the networks so as to carry vast volumes of simultaneous messages, as is already being demonstrated by the Internet.

Communication has also been enhanced by the use of satellites capable of beaming radio and television transmissions as well as telephone signals on a world coverage. Satellites, originally designed as defence spy systems, are also used to relay high-definition photographs of the earth, revealing weather data, other natural and human activity in amazing detail, as well as for space exploration.

These facilities have made it possible to link computers and for the individual to have almost instant access to a vast range of information and knowledge. The Internet therefore has a powerful potential for speeding up the intellectual processes of learning and research. Whether man has the ability to utilize this bewildering storehouse of knowledge remains to be seen, though it is highly likely that through the 21st century scientific research will intensify, aided by these tools of the communications revolution.

The computer revolution

The speed of increase in the power and the capacity of the computer has taken all those involved in the new industry by surprise. Yet there is a tendency in forecasters, when looking ahead through time spans of 25 years or longer, to imagine that giant leaps in technology will be achieved far sooner than proves to be the case.

H G Wells's essays in science fiction foresaw technical achievements which ultimately materialized long after the dates suggested. The same was true of George Orwell's *1984* and in the field of computer technology the brilliant science fiction author, Arthur C Clarke, estimated that a computer with artificial intelligence would be invented by the turn of the century. Rapid though computer development has been, it has not been that fast.

Computers will process the data that we feed them. Their data banks will be more reliable than human memory, though the human brain's ability to recognize things and situations and to recall from experience is so rapid and wide ranging that it must remain doubtful whether an artificial intelligence with that kind of ability will be installed in a computer within the next 25 years.

The body of knowledge stored in computers will undoubtedly go on expanding into increasing complexity. The computer will be able to sift undreamt-of volumes of data to provide the user with specific items of information bearing on specific subjects. It will be programmed so as to solve more and more complex data problems, but the succeeding steps towards artificial intelligence and human equivalence seem unlikely to be achieved before 2050.

The human brain, given enough experience, is able to resort to intuition and to jump illogically from one topic to another in unpredictable ways. Can we programme computers to be illogical and irrational? What would be the point of making an irrational computer, since we would not know which of its outpourings would be dependable and truthful?

Yet progress in this realm of computer power is still going to be impressive. Software will be designed to write software and any set of forecasts from now on has to face the question of the impact of computers on nearly every aspect of life, for good or ill. Computers will permeate most aspects of education, from the access to information and sources, to teaching programmes, group discussions and seminars as well as the advanced systems of scientific and educational research.

In this respect computer technology, with the Internet speeding up the access to and transfer of knowledge from research centre to research centre, from firm to firm, from country to country and from person to person, will maintain the tempo of technological advance and continuous industrial revolution. Perhaps the more important question is, can we harness such a growing body of technical change? Can we manage our lives, our lifestyles and our work practices to cope with these changes? Will these advances in production techniques and labour productivity result in our destroying more jobs than we create? And will the social problems arising from worklessness, job insecurity and the growing inequalities in society result in still further increases in violence and crime (and ultimately in revolt) or will society reorganize itself?

The continuous industrial revolution seems destined to generate a social revolution before the 21st century is out. It is by no means certain that man can cope with the accelerating pace of change.

Accelerating change

There has been an acceleration in the pace of change. The development of steam technology and its industrial application during the 19th century was relatively slow. By contrast, invention in the field of electronics and its application in a host of products since the Second World War shows a startling acceleration in the rate of technical progress.

As outlined in Chapter 3, the deepening of education, increase in the number of universities and graduates and expansion of research have all contributed to the spread of knowledge and the capacity to change. Change has also been stimulated by the growth of the international corporation and its ability to exploit new technology.

What we now call the 'communications revolution' has helped speed the transmission of ideas and changes in technology. The forecaster has, therefore, to recognize that the waves of new technology are forming a continuous flow of change.

The application of technology depends upon the ability of people to use new tools and new products. Although research lies at the heart of technical advance, we should recognize that the broadening of education plays its part in raising the ability and understanding of the potential labour force and the consumer. The introduction of compulsory education and the raising of the minimum school leaving age in most parts of the world has helped increase labour productivity. It has increased the stock of human skills and this has made it possible to introduce new technology at a faster pace.

The possible range of new products and ways of doing things is now greater than ever before. The whole body of human knowledge has expanded to such an extent that education and research is concentrated more and more in specialist compartments. Research has intensified within these disciplines and, in many forms of production, expertise is brought in from several specialist activities. Thus, in agriculture, for example, the farmer draws upon specialist advice from the chemist and biologist, the engineer and the financial adviser.

The increase in specialization and competition will tend to raise the flow of inventions and the possible number of new products, yet it has always been the case that the proportion of viable ideas is relatively small and in some instances an invention and patent may lie unused for many years before being taken up and brought to market.

The limits to change stem from two main sources: first, the limited spending power of the potential customer and, second, the limited ability of most humans to accept change. As a surviving animal man has demonstrated a remarkable ability to adapt to changes in the natural environment. In the absence of such compulsion, we tend to the conservative, resisting change except where change is so clearly beneficial as to be easy to make and accept.

The car, for example, quickly became an object of desire in the 20th century, as did the television set. The personal computer appears to be far less of an object of desire, even though its cost is relatively low compared with the car and TV at the corresponding stages of their development. Today, the range of items available to the consumer is greater than ever. What this means is that, given such wide choices, there are many more separate markets for our spending, so that the mass markets are less massive and more specialized.

Pipe dreams of a distant future seldom hit the mark. When looking 25 years or more ahead the forecaster seems invariably to exaggerate the pace of change. Even so, we can foresee the direction of change from the seeds which have already been planted. We know there is great concern about pollution and the wasteful use of fossil fuels. We know that there is very great research expenditure on developing highly fuel-efficient and 'clean' cars. We also know that the car is regarded as an 'essential' feature of modern life, extending personal freedom. This combination signals revolutionary changes in vehicle design throughout the 21st century to accommodate the growth in car ownership.

Changes to come

Continued dependence on the car makes the *computerized control of traffic* and road routes inevitable. Technology is already available to automate driving so that it would be feasible for a computer to take over control of the car on joining a motorway or major highway by locking onto an electronic road system which would control both the speed and position of the vehicle. This technology is likely to be introduced in cities and large towns in the advanced economies in areas of high population density, as well as on inter-city routes.

A number of pilot schemes of automated driving and traffic control are likely to be introduced in the first decades of the 21st century and networks are likely to be inaugurated in the rich, mature economies later in the century. Progress in this direction will continue through the century but coverage will still be far from complete at the century's end.

Such changes in transport systems will be accompanied by further advances in rail transport. The high speed networks will be expanded using the revolutionary *magnetic levitation* technology. A track is planned between Berlin and Hamburg adapting a technology dating from the 1920s. The 'Transrapid' train has no wheels and is propelled by magnetic fields. It clutches a concrete runway just as a runner glides along a curtain rail. This vehicle is capable of travelling at speeds of up to 300 mph, uses less energy than the French Train à Grande Vitesse (TGV) and is quieter. It is hoped that 14 million passengers a year will use the new route, should it be completed, reducing the train journey time from three hours to 55 minutes, taking passengers away from the airlines.

Japan is also working on similar technology. This creates a 10cm gap between the train and the track compared with only 10 mm in the German system. The larger gap is better suited to deal with earthquake risks. This system requires much more electricity so as to create very big magnetic fields.

These transit systems, if successful and adopted in other countries, will reduce potential demand for short-haul air routes. *Air travel* has been increasing rapidly and the continued strong growth in tourism as the populous developing nations become more affluent will raise challenging problems for the industry. Airport congestion is already making air travel uncomfortable. Security problems add to the delays. There is growing opposition to the expansion of airports and the airline operators are uncertain about the prospect of meeting expanding passenger numbers by commissioning bigger and bigger aircraft.

There will inevitably be significant advances in technology in this field. As with motor transport, fuel technology will be improved, incorporating new systems and fuels aimed at cutting fuel consumption and pollutant emissions. Hydrogen may well be in use by the end of the century. Airport congestion will require greater integration of transport systems to smooth the flow of passengers in and out of the area. In addition, engine design will be advanced so as to reduce noise.

There is likely to be renewed interest in *airship* design aimed at establishing an economic basis for both freight and passenger services at lower speeds. Passenger dissatisfaction with crowding and delays in aircraft and airports may result in a market for the slower and more spacious travel in airships, even at higher fares.

Man will also continue to venture into space. Bigger *manned space stations* will be brought into operation and the research making these developments possible will continue to generate useful by-products in the shape of new materials, tools and technology. Our knowledge and understanding of outer space and the origins of the universe will also expand and there must be some chance that, by the end of the 21st century, contact will have been established with other beings in other parts of the galaxy.

Research into *nuclear technology* will continue. Although there is growing opposition to the use of atomic power on environmental grounds, there is powerful support for maintaining and increasing nuclear capacity where conventional fuels are in short supply. Apart from the short-term risks from leaks from nuclear power plants, the long-term risks and cost of disposal and storage of nuclear waste, plus the costs of decommissioning nuclear power stations, has already led to decisions to phase out nuclear capacity in Sweden, and other countries may follow this route.

In the meantime, research will continue into the methodology and economics of nuclear fusion. Fusion, as opposed to fission, holds the promise of unleashing a much more abundant supply of energy. Scientists appear to have come close to success in the second half of the 20th century and there must be strong odds on a major advance in this sphere of technology before the end of the 21st century.

There will be major advances in our knowledge of the human body and in the structure of matter. *Genetic engineering* has made rapid advances and although there is powerful resistance on moral grounds to manipulation of human beings, there are many ways in which genetic engineering can be employed to improve crop fertility and animal husbandry, as well as to strengthen the constant fight against disease. In the fullness of time, genetic engineering is highly likely to be applied in attempts to eradicate certain human diseases and malfunctions. In this respect it is only a short step towards the creation of a test-tube baby. The technology will certainly be within man's grasp, though in this case the moral objections are likely to be sustained and the process will probably continue to be vetoed as a step too far.

Virtual reality is already in use as a form of entertainment. It also has a valuable potential as a means of training. The pictorial representation of things which we are unable to see, such as the insides of the human body, will, in this instance, help training in the medical field and in surgery. It has an important application in marketing, in that products can be displayed for the potential customer to 'inspect' at home via the television or Internet. Houses, for example, could be presented so that the potential buyer could 'walk' from room to room, see the views from the windows and study the environment. The technology of virtual reality will be enhanced and its capacity increased throughout the century.

In this connection, the continued growth in violence and crime, stemming to a large extent from the growing extremes between rich and poor in society, will lead to continued research into the *fight against crime*. The linkage of the TV screen and the computer has increased camera surveillance. Cable networks offer the opportunity to link property of all kinds to automated surveillance systems. Apart from surveillance, remote controls via the telephone will be expanded to lock and unlock premises, and computer systems will be devised to create 'intelligent' homes and buildings, controlling such things as temperature and air-conditioning, as well as security.

Robotics will also be extended into the home. A vacuum cleaner has been designed which will work its way over the room, identifying obstacles. Robots will be designed to take over more and more functions, so that labour will continue to be displaced in manufacturing and many boring and repetitive jobs will disappear. Robots could take over manual tasks in agriculture, such as the planting of rice, whilst repetitive clerical jobs, such as the entry of data into computers, could be automated.

The marriage of the computer and the telephone network has spawned the *Internet* and the next generation of technology in this field will simplify and speed up Internet procedures. Search will be reduced to a matter of seconds. The introduction of digital television opens the way for further major change, in that the computer and the Internet may be operated via the domestic television set.

The impact of the Internet on business will be far-reaching. Exploitation of the web by businesses will ultimately displace an entire range of middlemen, getting rid of inefficient distributors. Inventories will be reduced and deliveries speeded up. The cost savings will be substantial. In addition, the Internet will enable buyers to shop around and this will increase the downward pressure on prices.

The forecaster must therefore recognize that inflation will be held down by business-to-business operation of the Internet system. The cost savings are estimated to accrue at a rate of 0·25 per cent per annum, raising the rate of output growth of the advanced economies by a similar amount. Cheaper input prices will enable companies to raise their development and production plans.

A prime example of the likely cost savings is the link-up of the major US car producers to put their procurement needs onto a single electronic exchange. Spending $200 billions a year with thousands of suppliers in extended supply chains worth hundreds of billions of dollars each, the savings are expected to exceed $1000 per vehicle. This system is likely to be adopted by other heavy spending industry groups.

The rapid growth in business-to-business Internet transactions illustrated in Diagram 6.1 will increase pressure on profit margins. As a result, businesses will intensify their efforts to differentiate their products and services and to find new ways of connecting with customers to find out what they think and what they want.

The forecaster is therefore confronted with a business environment where change is accelerating and where new generations of products are being brought to market more frequently. Model changes will also be more frequent. It is seldom possible to predict the flow of new products coming onto the market with any certainty. Nevertheless, the forecaster must make allowance for the acceleration of technical change and assume that the competitors within a market will bring out new models with greater frequency and at more competitive prices.

The same assumptions have to be made about technical progress in the supply chain. Competition will stimulate research into the use and processing of materials, the use of energy, the manufacture of components and the use of labour. The forecasts have to take account of the speed of change on the supply side as well as the changes in demand.

Forecasting method

To assess the impact of technological investment on individual companies and a national economy it is instructive to study the pattern of technological

Diagram 6.1   The Web's worldwide business

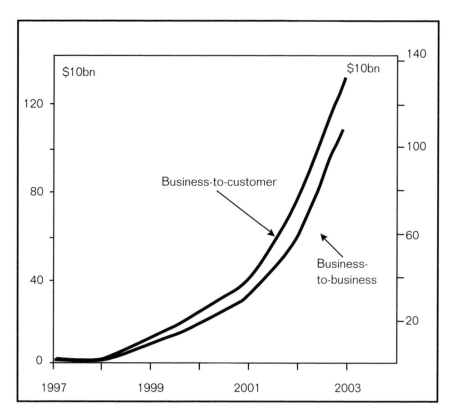

growth. Typically, this follows an S-shaped curve when a technological or technoeconomic capability is plotted against time. A similarly shaped curve would be obtained if it were possible to plot the same parameter against the cumulative investment in technology.

Diagram 6.2 plots the growth of the technical factor against the vertical scale over the life span of the 'S' curve. The horizontal line L marks the limit of the technology. The S curve can be conveniently considered in the following stages:

- A relatively slow initial growth in relation to the investment made. This is a period of high expectations, and often much disappointment.
- Very rapid growth and exploitation. This is the stage when new products proliferate and investment rises sharply over a relatively short period.
- A mature stage where increasingly large investments are required to obtain small incremental increases in performance.
- The emergence of new technology which will repeat the growth curve at a higher level of performance.

In forecasting the future impact of technology it is essential to bear in mind the stage which the technology has reached in the growth curve. Stage 1 often

Diagram 6.2   The technology 'S' curve

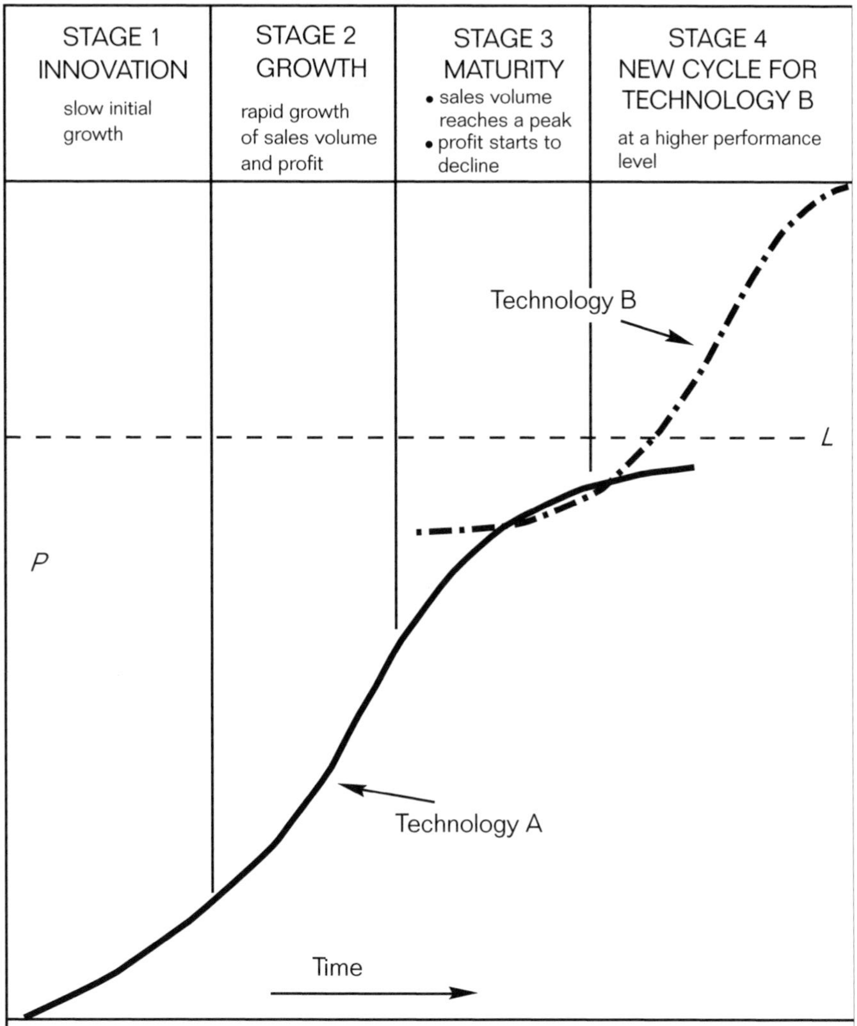

STAGE 1 INNOVATION	STAGE 2 GROWTH	STAGE 3 MATURITY	STAGE 4 NEW CYCLE FOR TECHNOLOGY B
slow initial growth	rapid growth of sales volume and profit	• sales volume reaches a peak • profit starts to decline	at a higher performance level

Technology B

— L

P

Technology A

Time

Notes: P may be a technical parameter (for example, lumens per watt for lighting) or a technoeconomic parameter (for example, cars/head of population);

L is a technical parameter indicating the limit for a technology set by the laws of nature.

covers a long period in time. Thus, although the technological capability has been identified, it is difficult to forecast when the period of rapid growth will commence. The evolution of electronics from the invention of radar in the 1930s and the birth of the computer in the 1940s has been extremely complex, embracing the pocket calculator, the wrist watch and a myriad of industrial and domestic applications. S curve follows S curve, the new technology linking with mature technology.

Where it is necessary to construct a forecast around technological change the following three factors should be considered:

- *technological capability* – the future technological or technoeconomic performance levels resulting from current and projected research and development (R&D) investment;
- *new technology* – the potential of new technologies in the products and markets traditionally based on other technologies; and
- *social need* – the degree to which forecasts based on the criteria of the past will need to be modified in view of the changing environment of technology, that is, concern with the physical environment, health and safety, depletion of non-renewable resources.

The generation of new technology is concentrated in the industrialized nations between which the knowledge gained flows at an increasing speed. The globalization of business ensures that those advances will infiltrate the developing economies. The national economy must therefore be viewed in a world context if the force of technological change is to be measured and analysed as part of a business forecast.

Conclusions

- The pace of technological change has accelerated into a permanent industrial revolution.
- The current phase is dominated by the stream of electronic developments and advances in biotechnology and genetic engineering.
- The communications revolution is part of the new wave of industrial development and will contribute via the Internet to repressing price inflation.
- The possible range of new products and ways of doing things is now greater than ever before. The forecaster must allow for new generations of products being brought to market more frequently.
- It is not possible to predict the flow of new products with any certainty, but the forecaster must assume that competitors will bring out new models more frequently and at more competitive prices.
- The pattern of technological growth follows a series of S curves and a technological forecast must identify the phases of the product's growth and the factors determining the likelihood of success of an investment in research and development.

Sources

Victorian Engineering (Rolt).

The Power of the Machine (Buchanan).

Preparing for the Twenty First Century (Kennedy).

The Long Wave in the World Economy (Tylecote).

Remaking Eden (Silver).

7 SPENDING POWER, PROFITS AND THE MARKET

The individual firm has no control over the spending power of its customers and potential markets. Spending power in a national economy is dominated by households and individual consumers. Personal income is therefore the most important element in spending power, wages and salaries making the biggest contribution.

Producers of capital goods sell principally to other businesses. Spending power in those markets is largely generated by company profits and to a lesser extent by funds raised from the banks and the stock markets.

Government spending is another source of spending power, as are foreign firms which make up the potential export market.

Forecasting wages and salaries

The levels of pay are largely determined by supply and demand. Where there is a shortage of skilled labour, pay rates will tend to rise faster than average. Across the labour market as a whole, supply is reflected in the figures for the number of people unemployed and looking for work. Demand is indicated by the number of unfilled job vacancies.

The balance between unemployment and unfilled vacancies gives a measure of the pressures in the labour market, excessive unemployment tending to hold pay rates down. An excess of unfilled vacancies will tend to force pay settlements up at a faster pace. The national measures of unemployment and vacancies are far from perfect. Social security provision, which varies from country to country, will have a bearing on whether an unemployed person is looking for work. In some cases persons claiming and in receipt of unemployment benefit are counted, the total being used as a measure of unemployment.

The reality may be different, since there will be large numbers of people who want work but who are not in receipt of unemployment benefit. Women, for example, who have left the labour force to raise children, may want to find paid employment but will not be included in the count of the unemployed. In addition, many older people, having been made redundant ahead of retirement, may be available for work without being counted as unemployed.

Entitlement to unemployment benefit is far from uniform between countries. Unemployment benefit is more generous in some countries than in others and the length of time for which the benefit is paid varies by wide margins. These problems of measurement and definition invalidate comparisons between countries and the forecaster must study the terms of the specific national labour market in which he is interested. The problem is eased to some extent in that the International Labour Office (ILO), an organ of the United Nations, uses a standardized measure of unemployment based on those people available for work and looking for work.

However, whatever the measures available to the analyst, some indications of change can be extracted from a monthly series of figures taken from a single source. The national statistics are presented in both a seasonally adjusted and an unadjusted form and both the unemployment and job vacancy figures in seasonally adjusted form should be used in the analysis. The unfilled vacancy figures are compiled from various sources and these vary from country to country. Job advertising provides a barometer of demand for higher paid staff but for the labour market as a whole data are collected from both government and private employment agencies.

Employment and unemployment statistics lag behind the changes in the economy at large. Changes in production and order books will determine whether or not a firm will need to employ more or fewer people. These decisions are reflected some months later in the figures for employment, unemployment and unfilled vacancies. Thus, if the forecaster has a finger on the pulse of what is happening in terms of spending and output in the economy, it will be possible to anticipate the next moves in the labour market and the likely changes in pay settlements and pay rates.

Employers will usually resist laying off workers where a downturn in business is thought to be temporary. Economies can be made by reducing overtime working and the national unemployment figures tend to lag economic activity to a greater extent than is the case with the job vacancy figures. Thus the relationship between the unemployment and vacancy figures is usually out of balance for a short period at turning points in the economy when output begins to accelerate or decelerate.

The forecaster will follow the obvious course of relating changes in pay to changes in the net demand for labour. The historical record will show a relationship and when the monthly seasonally adjusted figures for both series are plotted on a chart, the length of time lag between the labour series and pay series will be clear by inspection. It will be necessary to take the figures back for two cycles or more – perhaps as much as 15 years – to get a reliable estimate of time lag and the ratio of the change in pay to the change in the net demand for labour. The series might show, for example, that after a time lag pay rates rise by an additional 2 per cent for every 1 per cent in the net demand for labour.

At this point it is essential to keep in mind that this kind of relationship is not set in stone. Minute changes in society take place all the time and over a period of years these combine to form a significant change in behaviour. During the 1990s, the world economy left behind the inflationary psychology of the previous decades and moved into a deflationary phase. Job insecurity, having increased over a long period, began to assert a larger influence on pay settlements, and patterns of employment changed. There was a greater use of part-time employment and more work was contracted out. In addition, there was growing downward pressure on prices, which bore down on profit margins, forcing employers to trim costs.

As a result, pay inflation declined and the old relationship between the demand for labour and pay levels changed. Pay has been rising less than predicted by the relationship observed over the previous cycles. This is illustrated in Diagram 7.1, showing unemployment and wage earnings in the UK over a 20-year period from the late 1970s.

Diagram 7.1   Unemployment and earnings

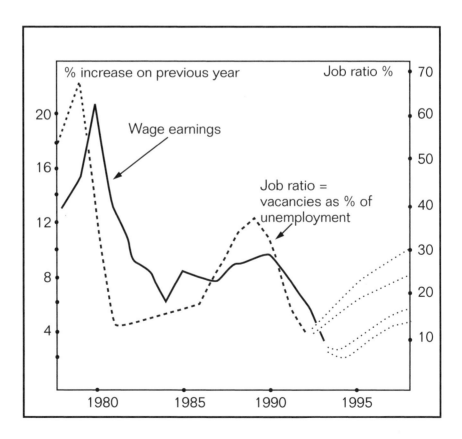

The annual increase in wage earnings is plotted against the ratio of job vacancies as a percentage of the number of unemployed. The job ratio appears to lead the change in wage earnings by a year or so. The predicted change from 1993 shows a rise in the job ratio, that is, a fall in the labour surplus, and an acceleration in wage inflation to over 10 per cent. This was in the wake of the devaluation of sterling in 1992 and from the evidence of previous devaluations it was widely assumed that cost and price inflation would be forced higher. This did not happen and, although my forecast of a rise in the job ratio was correct, there was no matching rise in pay inflation. The old relationship had been broken and, as noted above, the world economic environment had moved in a deflationary direction, marking a significant revolution away from the inflationary environment of the previous 30 years.

Although the relationship has changed, it is still the case that changes in the net demand for labour are reflected, with a time lag, in the rate of change in the rates of pay, and any forecast of employment income has to start from that basic position.

Using the national income accounts, the forecast percentage change in pay rates can be applied to the cash value of total wages and salaries in estimating total employment income. Some adjustment has to be made for the cyclical effect on income since in 'good' times, when the economy is expanding at an above-average rate, there is more overtime working paid for at premium rates, plus higher bonuses. Total employment income therefore rises faster than wage rates. Conversely, where the economy grows at a below-average pace, slipping towards recession, total employment income rises more slowly than wage rates. This difference is known in the economist's jargon as 'wage drift'.

The build-up of spending power

Total household and personal income is made up of other items and in the mature economies the approximate proportions of income sources are as shown in Table 7.1. To establish the level of spending power the forecaster should concentrate on cash flow and ignore the build-up of assets in the shape of employers' contributions to pension schemes and national social security taxation. The gross receipts shown in Table 7.1 represent cash received before deductions for taxation and employees' contributions to contractual savings towards pensions and insurance. Net income, or disposable income, is shown in Table 7.2.

There are wide differences in the national patterns of taxation, social security taxes being notably high in most European countries. In the USA, income tax varies between states and the total of federal and state income taxes has to be deducted in arriving at the disposable funds total. Contractual savings also

Table 7.1   Household and personal income (%)

Income from employment	55
Income from self-employment	10
Pensions and social security benefits	30
Investment income	5
Gross income	100

vary, depending upon the extent to which pensions are paid out of general taxation.

Some estimate has also to be made of voluntary savings. Saving in some countries is volatile and the evidence suggests that, when unemployment is rising and an economy is headed into recession, households become more cautious, increasing what I call 'cash' savings in deposit accounts. The analyst must also be wary of the national income estimates of savings which are arrived at by deducting the estimated total of spending from the estimated total of disposable income. Relatively small errors in the spending and income totals can result in extremely large errors in the savings estimate.

Theoretically, the problem could be solved by recording the flows into the various outlets for savings. The results, however, are not convincing since the range of possible outlets is wide. Movements into and out of bank and other accounts, purchases of securities in other countries and attempted tax avoidance and tax evasion make it nearly impossible to compile an accurate measure of all the flows.

Forecasting the miscellaneous sources of income and deductions for a national economy is less difficult, since tax rates and social security contributions and benefits tend to change gradually, the changes usually being signposted well in advance.

Another feature to be taken into account is the use of credit. Debt is constantly being repaid or rolled over and the net increase in the use of credit

Table 7.2   Disposable household and personal income (%)

Gross income	100
less income and social security taxes	17
less contractual savings	8
equals disposable funds	75

fluctuates with the level of interest rates. The interest rate cycle generates stronger growth in lending as rates fall, and vice versa. Consumer credit therefore sharpens the cycle in household cash flow and is directly related to spending, particularly on durables.

The sum of these factors provides a measure of the prospective change in household and personal spending power, accounting for some 80 to 85 per cent of national domestic income. The profits of companies and publicly owned enterprises account for most of the remaining 15 to 20 per cent.

The money value of spending power must also be converted to adjust for inflation to obtain a measure of the rate of change in real terms. The rate of growth in current prices is divided by the rate of change in consumer prices. For example, should the money value of spending power rise by 5 per cent per annum and consumer prices by 2 per cent per annum, then the increase in real terms is given by $1.05 \div 1.02 = 1.029$, that is, 2.9 per cent per annum.

Forecasting profits

In the economy as a whole the national income is measured (as outlined in Chapter 1) in terms of its factor incomes. It is possible, therefore, to estimate aggregate profits earned in the domestic economy by deducting income from employment and rent from national income (see Table 7.3). Profits are volatile, being the difference between total revenue and total costs. We are not concerned at this point with forecasting an individual company's profits but with forecasting profits in aggregate so as to obtain a measure of the changes in spending power of the domestic business market.

Table 7.3 Factor incomes in the national economy

Total domestic income
less income from employment
less income from self-employment
less rent
equals total profits

A forecast of the general trend in profits and the cycle provide an indicator of the market for capital goods. As a rule of thumb, investment spending lags as much as a year behind the changes in company profits and cash flow. That lag stems from the time it takes for the board to recognize from its monthly or quarterly management accounts that cash flow is going to be better or worse than anticipated. If a decision is then taken to increase or reduce capital spending commitments there is a further time lag as plans are revised and orders placed or cancelled.

Profits are difficult to forecast, not least because of the uncertain nature of the statistics. The profits series shown in national income accounts are frequently revised and by wide margins. The problem arises partly from problems of definition and also from the sampling of companies. The continued growth of multinational corporations raises problems in disentangling the profits earned in a particular country from the group accounts. In addition, companies do not operate within a uniform accounting year; neither do they necessarily produce quarterly accounts. In any event the accounts are not available until around three months after the company year end, and in some cases longer.

Collecting and collating the data is obviously difficult and the problems are exacerbated by differences in accounting standards between countries and complexities arising from taxation, allowances and – in some cases – subsidies. The official statisticians have the task of estimating 'gross trading profits' for the whole company sector, earned solely within the country. Trading profits are struck before subtracting taxation, interest and depreciation charges.

The cyclical fluctuation in profits is greater than in the economy as a whole. One reason is that government spending has a mild stabilizing effect on the economy whilst the full effect of changes in interest rates and exchange rates falls with greater force on the company sector. This feature can be seen when the changes in costs and prices relevant to the company sector are compared with the corresponding changes for the whole economy.

The company profits share of national income tends to go up in periods when unemployment is rising and the weakness of the labour market depresses employment incomes. When the demand for labour is buoyant, employment incomes take a higher share of national income.

This approach generates another route to forecasting the cyclical changes in profits and the timing can be understood by following the reactions of a business to sharp changes in interest rates. These effects are magnified in the dominant quoted company sector since share prices react quickly to interest rate changes. The board will be sensitive to falls in the company's share price following a hike in interest rates and will tend to act to reduce costs as soon as possible. In the meantime, cuts made by customer firms will reduce the company's sales and profits. After a time lag in which cost savings are put into effect – principally through reducing employment – the haemorrhaging of profits is halted. Profits then begin to recover and share prices improve, producing a paradox in that rising unemployment is accompanied by a rising stock market.

Thus a combination of approaches will help to form a more confident profile of profits. That in turn will help generate a forecast of the market for capital goods lagging both the profits forecast and the forecast for the much larger market for consumer goods and services.

The impact of foreign trade

All economies are engaged in world trade. The USA, with a continental economy, is more self-sufficient than most countries, whereas the Netherlands has far higher proportions of imports and exports with the rest of the world.

The forecaster must take account of the contribution that exports make to the national market and also the extent to which imports supply the total market. Both exports and imports are sensitive to movements in exchange rates. For many goods and services, selling prices are determined by the domestic market and the international trader has in most cases to fix his prices according to what the market will bear.

Thus, where a currency is significantly overvalued, the exporter will receive less in its domestic currency and its profits are depressed since it is unlikely that it will be able to make matching cost reductions in the short run. At the same time imports are stimulated by the overvaluation of the currency and domestic firms will tend to lose share of the market to the foreign exporter.

This is another feature bearing on the national profit level which has to be built into the profit forecast. Swings in the international trade balance are reflected in the profits cycle, tending to magnify its volatility. The overvaluation or undervaluation of a currency does not persist indefinitely and changes in the interest rate differentials between countries make an impact, with time lags, on the flows and profitability of international trade.

The black economy

No analysis of the national market of an economy is complete without some recognition and assessment of the unrecorded transactions which make up the shadow, or unobserved, black economy. Every country has a black economy and the very existence of taxation guarantees that some of the citizenry will attempt to evade taxation in a range of unrecorded activities and spending.

There is a large element of 'moonlighting', where people have a second job and payment in many cases is in cash. Many unemployed people also take on jobs for cash to supplement their social security incomes. The common feature of the black economy is that payment is received without the raising of invoices. There is also an element of barter which goes unrecorded which in less developed economies is of large proportions.

In the advanced economies some indication of the existence and extent of the black economy is contained in the aggregate national income figures. The expenditure method of estimating the national income almost invariably exceeds the estimate derived from the income method. A large part of the incomes total is derived from the income tax returns, whereas the spending total is largely made up from surveys of household expenditure. Unrecorded income generated from the black economy is largely spent and partly saved and those cash expenditures show up in recorded receipts.

The black economy is for the most part made up of service activities rather than manufacture, and the principle sources are as follows:

- home maintenance and improvement;
- catering, guest houses and entertainment;
- car maintenance and taxis;
- market trading and scrap dealing;
- commission agencies;
- hairdressing; and
- prostitution.

Criminal activities generate a large part of the black economy income, principally via drug trafficking, theft, fraud, money laundering and smuggling.

It is not surprising, therefore, that these unrecorded activities contribute to a black economy equivalent to 10 per cent or more of the world's developed economies. Apart from the discrepancy between the official estimates of total income and total spending, the demand for cash provides further clues as to the scale of the black economy. With the growth of banking and the use of credit cards, the need for cash currency declines. The evidence, however, contradicts this and demonstrates that there has been a growing demand for cash to meet the transaction requirements of the unrecorded economy.

The national markets as described in the official national income statistics are generally understated. Italy, where the black economy is of large proportions, now incorporates an estimate of the black economy in its official statistics and some countries make modest adjustments to allow for underrecording. In the sample surveys of household spending, where the members of the household record the details of their spending over a period of time, spending on alcohol, gambling, confectionery and sex are underrecorded. The extent of the underrecording can be checked from the national statistics generated by sales or value added tax receipts and police records of prostitution. The official statistics are adjusted for these discrepancies.

In one other respect the national accounts understate the level of activity, in that domestic work is not credited with any value. Housework, gardening and house maintenance on the do-it-yourself (DIY) basis are disregarded, whereas in fact they create a value. If the family members did not carry out this unpaid work but depended on paid help, that help would feature in the national income accounts – unless, that is, the work was paid for in cash and not declared. If all wives divorced their husbands and demanded to be paid a housekeeper's salary, the national income would be substantially bigger.

For forecasting purposes, where the black economy is a significant part of the market, as in the case of house maintenance and improvement, some addition should be made to the official figures for spending of the sector. Materials bought for carrying out the work via the black economy and DIY will be recorded in the sales ledgers of the suppliers. The labour element is not recorded and it is to this extent that the sector market is understated.

It can be argued that the forecaster should ignore the black economy since it is a permanent feature and the rate of change from year to year in the recorded economy would be the same if the unrecorded economy were to be added to the series. This, however, does not make allowance for the impact of the business cycle.

When the economy is buoyant and spending and output are rising at an above-average rate, households have more cash and will spend more in the black economy. At the same time, unemployment is likely to be falling and the number of people operating in the black economy will be marginally lower and their asking prices will be higher. In the downswing of the cycle, incomes are squeezed and unemployment tends to rise. There is less money available for spending in the black economy whilst there will be more people offering their services in that market. The prices asked will be forced lower and there are likely to be greater cyclical swings in the revenues of the black economy than in the recorded economy.

There are many 'guesstimates' of the size of the black economy and, given all the uncertainties, any of these estimates must be treated with caution. Nevertheless, they should not be ignored. The consensus of the various estimates suggests that the size of the black economy in relation to the relevant GDP official figures is shown in Table 7.4. The Russian figure is put at around 100 per cent of the published GDP figures.

Competitive forces

There is a distinct advantage in building up a profile of a national market as a whole. The exercise provides a number of cross-checks which serve to improve the reliability of the components and to reduce the uncertainties.

The single business is clearly unable to control the broad market into which it sells and it is exceptional for a giant firm to establish a controlling monopoly for more than a brief period. In wartime, governments may authorize, or help establish, price controls where shortages would otherwise tend to force costs and prices up. Farm prices and commodity prices have also been controlled in wartime.

Table 7.4   Black economy as % of GDP

Austria	10	Japan	5
Belgium	15	Netherlands	10
Canada	10	Norway	10
Denmark	11	Spain	18
Finland	9	Sweden	13
France	9	Switzerland	6
Germany	10	UK	9
Ireland	9	US	8
Italy	25		

In normal business conditions every industry and every firm is both directly and indirectly in competition for its share of a specific market within the national market. It is not sufficient to limit the analysis of the competition to the single product's market.

We have to recognize that all businesses are in competition for the potential customer's spending power. Inevitably, some items, such as paying the rent or the mortgage, have the highest priority. Once the essentials of life have been budgeted for there will be many competing claims on the household's spending power. The prospective purchase of a car may be in competition with the booking of a holiday. The forecaster must therefore take account of a wide spectrum of competitive forces in defining specific markets within the range of national spending power.

Conclusions

- Employment income is the most important element in spending power and the national market.
- The net demand for labour provides a measure of the pressure for change in wage earnings, with a time lag and a cyclical pattern.
- Income from employment typically accounts for 55 per cent of household pre-tax income.
- Estimates and forecasts of spending power should be based on the household cash flow; that is, after deduction of taxes and contractual savings.
- Allowance must also be made for changes in the use of credit.
- To forecast the changes in total national market an adjustment has to be made for price inflation to establish a forecast in volume terms.
- Changes in company profits lead changes in investment spending by an average of up to a year.
- Estimates of profit incomes in national accounts are erratic and subject to major revisions. Nevertheless, by constructing estimates using the swings

in the national business cycle it is possible to generate forecasts of business spending power.

- The profit cycle is sharper than the cycle for the national economy, as is also the case with the changes in export markets.
- Some allowance must be made for the unrecorded, black economy, which is equivalent to around 10 per cent of GDP in the advanced economies.
- Estimates for the building industry should contain an allowance for the black economy, which tends to have a sharp cyclical movement, exacerbating changes in the total market.

Sources

The national income accounts provide income data on an annual and quarterly basis. Wage earnings are reported on a monthly basis.

Data covering unemployment and vacancies are available on a monthly basis. Employment data are also published on a monthly basis in most countries.

The United Nations and the OECD publish regular surveys of national economies giving a range of background statistics. The OECD publishes short-term forecasts.

Private forecasting bodies also publish material covering incomes, spending power and market aggregates.

PART 2

UNDER THE FIRM'S CONTROL

8 LONG-TERM STRATEGY AND INVESTMENT

Much of a firm's forecasting work will be concerned with the outcome of its investment decisions. Major investment projects originate in most cases from the firm's long-term strategy and plans.

Large corporations tend to review their plans from year to year, imposing a discipline throughout the major components of the company. Plans, however, are constructed to meet the firm's objectives. Thus the starting point for planning and investment has to be a review of the firm's performance and operating ratios and a set of decisions on where the board of directors wishes to take the business.

The strategic plan may lay down targets for the return of capital employed, the growth in earnings per share and dividends per share, as well as the prospective share price. It may also include targets for market share of its various products and services and make provision for product development and new products.

None of these decisions should be taken in a vacuum. If targets are to be realistic and attainable, allowance has to be made for changes in the operating environment outlined in previous chapters. If, for example, price inflation and interest rates have been high, the firm will probably have set a high target rate of return on capital employed. But if there is evidence of a change in trend towards low inflation and interest rates, then the target rate of return has to be lowered. If not, the business may suffer from underinvestment, since prospective investment projects will show a lower potential return than the targets laid down by the board.

Setting long-term strategy

We have stressed the importance of knowing as much as possible about the past in order to identify the trends and changes in trends bearing on the economy. The same applies to the individual business. Directors and managers, having experience of the company's activities, markets and performance over a number of years, will have some familiarity with the firm's operating ratios. Yet the complexity of a large company means that it is necessary to spell out the history of the components of business over the past decade. This is essential to draw out the strengths and weaknesses of the enterprise and to identify where successful and profitable expansion can be made.

Without that history it will not be possible to set realistic targets. Moreover, those targets must be consistent. The likelihood is that the company may have to generate bigger annual increments of cash to finance the investment needed to meet investment plans. This will raise questions as to the strength of the competition and what should be assumed about the plans of the competitors. These questions need to be answered to establish whether it is feasible to raise profit margins, for example.

Thus the individual company needs to analyse its own operating ratios and performance in order to formulate its strategy and plans for future development and expansion, and to maintain or increase its profitability. Apart from its internal requirements, a company will need to adopt the same methods of analysis in order to study the performance of its rivals and to evaluate other companies for the purposes of mergers and acquisitions.

Return on capital employed

One of the first steps in analysis is to measure the efficiency of management in relation to return on capital. The management of capital can only be judged in terms of return achieved on that capital. The results of earlier decisions and day-to-day management are ultimately reflected in profits, and the return on capital is probably the most dependable measure we have of the success of management.

Thus, for the company to decide upon a target return on capital and a certain prospective level of earnings per share, it will be necessary for past performance and return on capital to be analysed with some care. Similarly, the analyst will need to pay considerable attention to identifying the reasons for apparent success or failure.

It is important to distinguish between return on capital as a whole and return on assets from the point of view of the shareholder. In order to judge the efficiency of management, it is necessary to examine the return obtained on the total stock of assets. How those assets are financed is immaterial. For example, where targets need to be set within a company for its various operating divisions, it will be essential to distinguish the assets under the control of each division and to ask the management of each division to be judged according to the return achieved on those assets. From the point of view of internal control and comparisons, it is necessary to have estimates of the gross return on gross assets. Similarly, in order to make comparisons between firms, either within one industry or within the economy as a whole, it is still important to measure the respective efficiency in the use of assets.

The concept of the gross return on gross assets can be thought of as the economic yardstick. Since the analyst is concerned primarily with the question of efficiency in the management of assets, the return measured after depreciation and before tax on the total body of assets, with fixed assets valued at replacement cost, will give the kind of yardstick required for inter-firm comparison and also for comparisons within the firm.

Although for the purposes of economic assessment, it is irrelevant how assets have been financed, it is still essential to analyse the development of the return on shareholders' funds and to set targets in terms of earnings per share. Growth in the return on shareholders' net assets is ultimately the most important single factor leading to growth in the share price. The maximization of earnings per share for shareholders will be the prime consideration both of the company and of the security analyst.

The target rate of return on gross assets may be determined in a number of ways. A convenient method is to set the target at twice the long-term rate of interest. This approach is logical in that it reflects the rate of price inflation and the risk inherent in equity investment. The long-term rate of interest is a proxy for the price of long-term funds. Historically, the interest rate reflects not only the supply and demand for funds but changes in the value of money as reflected in the rate of inflation. In settling a target rate of return the board must make some assumption to cover any change in the rate of inflation through the plan period, and other factors, such as government funding needs, which will be reflected in the interest rate.

Whilst this approach allows for uncertainty and risk, the board is likely to adopt a wider spectrum of target rates to allow for the range of risk attached to different investment projects. Where investment is fundamental to the business, the target rate will be set at a lower rate than for uncertain and more risky projects. Thus twice the long-term interest rate may be appropriate for core, or fundamental, investment but higher target rates will be imposed for cyclical and more volatile investment projects.

At the other extreme, some investments must be undertaken to comply with health and safety legislation regardless of its contribution to profit and cash flow. There is little point in laying down a target rate of return for this kind of outlay.

The important distinction between the different measures of return is that the return on total capital is a key indicator so far as judging the efficiency of industrial management is concerned, whereas the net return on shareholders' funds is the key indicator in assessing management effectiveness in the interests of shareholders. The second indicator will be dependent upon the first, but the whole question of financing and capital leverage (or gearing) is a subject for separate analysis. Within the company the managers of individual divisions should be concerned with maximizing the return on total assets.

The question of maximizing this return in terms of rewards for shareholders is a problem for the board. The finance department, or division, must have the responsibility for deciding how assets are to be financed. Risk analysis and financial analysis belong at the centre of the corporation rather than with the divisional management. It is the board's central responsibility to determine the targets for return on equity.

Planning

The planner's task is to map out the course of the business through the period for which the board has set the firm's objectives. The horizon year may be set for five years ahead or longer in the case of the multinational corporation and the users of long-lived assets.

Forecasting to meet these horizon year targets entails a careful study of previous trends and the analysis of the markets in which the business is likely to operate. Certain assumptions will be required about society at large, such as changing tastes and fashions, changes in the level of purchasing power and changes in population structures. Changes in working practices will need to be analysed and allowances made for changing technology.

These considerations can be judged only against a long time scale. In general, the first attempt to construct a forecast along these lines will involve the identification of underlying trends and the estimation of the likely trend level to be attained at the end of the forecast period. Yet this can only be a beginning in the forecasting work for, in many instances, straight-line projections will be quite inadequate for planning purposes.

For example, in a cyclical industry, if a forecast is made starting from the top of one business cycle and the trend is correctly forecast to the top of the next business cycle, a plan based on such a forecast could have disastrous results. The fact that the cycle begins to move downwards at the outset of the plan period means that there will be a shortfall of profits and cash flow in the early years of the period. Thus the cash resources will not be available to meet the planned investment in new productive resources. This is illustrated in Diagram 8.1.

In a cyclical business, therefore, it is necessary to construct a forecast for the plan period year by year. In practice the great majority of businesses have some kind of cyclical experience. When profits are plotted out year by year over a ten-year period, a cyclical pattern becomes apparent and it is quite exceptional for a business not to display such characteristics. Even a rapidly growing and successful business still shows signs of a cyclical fluctuation about its strongly rising trend.

It is not only those industries most dependent upon credit conditions which

Diagram 8.1 A profit forecast

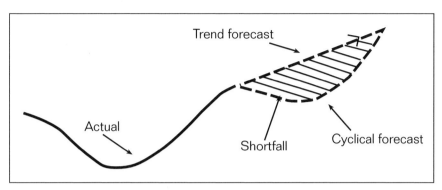

display cyclical patterns. Housebuilding, motor vehicles and other consumer durables are subject to sharp swings in demand owing to changes in the cost of bank credit and hire-purchase finance.

Capital goods industries are subject to sharp cyclical fluctuations in demand as a result of fluctuations in profits in general. Investment, by and large, is financed from profits and swings in profitability inevitably lead to swings in the pattern of investment spending.

Forecasting assumptions and scenarios

The firm's plan is a route aimed at meeting its objectives. If the plan is to be effective and to have a realistic chance of achieving the targets set by the board, it must be based on a set of assumptions about the future. Those assumptions will shape the forecasts of the business environment and of the firm's achievements.

Every forecast hinges upon its underlying assumptions. From the user's point of view it is essential to be aware of what those assumptions are. The business has to look at itself within its national context and the national scene must be set in a world context. A rigorous set of forecasts ought, therefore, to be derived from a set of international and national assumptions embracing the following items for the forecast period. See Table 8.1.

It may also be necessary where there is a longer time horizon to make assumptions about changes in the size and age structure of the population. For some firms it will be necessary to look at social pressures which may result in legislation in such areas as female equality and discrimination on grounds of sex, race and age, as well as environmental factors.

That framework of assumptions will shape the broad forecasts covering the firm's markets. Major companies may have computerized models of the international and national economies. The majority will not, and may be

Table 8.1   The business environment assumptions (year-to-year changes, %)

International	World output
	World trade value and volume
	The exchange rate
	Import and export prices
National	Monetary policy, interest rates and money supply
	Wage rates, wages and salaries
	Consumer credit
	Personal income tax rates
	Social security taxes
	Indirect tax rates
	The household savings ratio
	Corporate tax rates
	Public sector current spending
	Public sector capital spending
	The fiscal deficit (or surplus)

dependent upon the forecasts generated by professional forecasting firms and institutions.

I take a guarded view of the reliability of computerized models ('econometrics' in the jargon language). As we have noted, rubbish in equals rubbish out, since many statistical series have large potential sampling errors. In most cases the series are heavily revised from time to time. This means that the relationships identified from the historical evidence are not generally robust. In any event, relationships and trends change over time. The models must therefore be used with caution. The answers are likely to be in the right ball park, but every series must be assessed for reliability, uncertainty and risk.

The computerized model comes into its own, however, in testing the significance of the differing assumptions. It may be important, for example, to know how the forecasts differ if interest rates are assumed to be two percentage points higher or lower. The model can be used in this way to generate a sensitivity analysis and the differences in results thrown up by varying assumptions will be highly significant and dependable, whether or not the model itself is perfectly accurate.

Sensitivity analysis can be used by testing individual assumptions rather than by changing several assumptions at the same time. In this way features which are likely to be critical in formulating the business plan can be subjected to a sensitivity analysis. The differences in results thrown up will illustrate the riskiness of particular plan decisions.

This exercise must not be undertaken without applying a commonsense approach to the mix of assumptions. A set of forecasting assumptions must be mutually consistent. It would be patently wrong to assume a rapid rise in money supply and a low rate of inflation, for example.

The permutation of assumptions and application of sensitivity analysis form part of the technique of scenario forecasting. The preparation of consistent sets of different scenarios is time-consuming, but it is intellectually more satisfying to approach planning in this way and to provide the decision takers with different stories. In the energy markets, for example, it is instructive to look at scenarios illustrating the impact of developing different combinations of energy sources, as well as scenarios where oil supplies are disrupted by wars.

The majority of firms will not be confronted by such an exciting range of plausible scenarios. Moreover, the decision takers will not have unlimited reserves of time and intellectual energy to pursue all legitimate lines of enquiry. In most cases the board will be looking for a 'best bet' set of forecasts with a high and a low set of answers to illustrate sensitivity and risk. The planner has to take a practical approach to the use of limited resources.

This does not mean, however, that a critical factor which could have a major impact on the firm's prospects should be ignored because it is not part of the 'best bet' scenario. We are confronted by unforeseen shocks in the world economy more often than is generally recognized. The future must therefore be approached with humility and the planner must ask many questions about what might go wrong in the economic environment and decide whether there are any outsiders in the race which have to be brought to the board's attention, even if the odds against are fairly long.

The Delphi technique

There is another approach to formulating and testing assumptions which should be considered in a major planning exercise. Known as the Delphi technique, the idea is derived from Delphi itself, which was held by the Greek states to be the centre of the world. Delphi was independent of the Greek city states and from the 8th century BC the temple of Apollo at Delphi was the site of the oracle. The oracle was consulted about important decisions by visitors throughout the Greek world for the next thousand years.

A supplicant would put his question to the oracle for a fee or donation, which could be very substantial. The function of oracle was performed by a number of aged virgins who put themselves into a trance by chewing bay leaves. The client was received in a hollow beneath the temple (still visible today) and the unintelligible reply was interpreted by the duty priests who proceeded to transcribe the answer onto a lead tablet, the answers being composed in Greek hexameters with a copy kept on file.

Today's consultative Delphi process is designed to produce a range of answers to a large number of questions, the only common link with antiquity being the anonymity of the various oracles. The system is used to test the validity of assumptions and scenarios for use in the planning and forecasting process. The organizer and controller of the consultative exercise must design a number of questions relating to the project in question which may include items about the world economy, national economies, industries and markets, government policies, social and technological change and so on.

The resultant questionnaire will require a numerical response in some cases as well as comment. The oracles will be members of the firm who may be involved in policy making or management and in various specialist functions, such as finance or research. The key point of the exercise is that the respondents do not consult and remain anonymous from one another.

The advantage of the technique is that the individual is able to express views in an uninhibited way. Where questions are discussed in committee, junior and less experienced members may well hold back for fear of appearing foolish, or where the boss is a dominant character whose views are seldom disputed.

The respondents' replies are collated by the organizer and circulated to the Delphi group with a repetition of the questions. These may include new ideas or modified questions generated by the first round of replies. This process is repeated several times, depending on the importance of the forecasting exercise and the time constraints. The value of the exercise lies in the opening up of questions to individuals from different disciplines who will not be steeped in old dogma and who may have views radically different from the accepted wisdom. The end result will be a range of assumptions for various scenarios and a range of forecasting numbers. These will give a more dependable appraisal of both risks and opportunities.

At this point I must give a word of warning. The technique can work well within an organization. The contributors are likely to honour the timetable so that each round can be completed according to schedule. However, on one occasion I attempted to run a Delphi exercise open to a large number of contributors from other firms. The exercise failed because the contributors could not be compelled to meet their obligations. For various reasons the response rate fell away and it seemed likely that some volunteers joined for what they hoped to get out of the exercise without any commitment to putting something in.

In a well-run and successful Delphi exercise there is likely to be a valuable contribution of ideas which have not been discussed before. There will be surprises and in many instances, preconceived ideas will be dropped and the generally accepted wisdom modified. The technique is used to test opinions in research work where success rates are uncertain and budgets are constrained. Product development and investment projects can also be tested.

Product development

Investment in new products and in replacement and additions to productive capacity are all within the firm's control and account for a large part of its forecasting requirement.

Product development is partly dictated by competition: as competitors update their product ranges the chances are that market shares within the industry will change. Thus all firms within the industry run the risk of losing market share unless they update their products and introduce new lines.

The forecaster has to allow for a continuous process of product change and innovation within the industry. The starting point for the forecast has to be an analysis of the long-term trend for the market as a whole and an estimate of the future trend, making allowance for the major international and national factors bearing on the market. Having established a forecast for the market as a whole, that forecast must be broken down into its component products and component competitors.

The results will be more dependable if the forecasts are made from the top down, rather than built up to a total from separate forecasts of the components. Particular caution should be used in estimating market share. Marketing people are understandably biased towards optimism and there is a natural tendency for marketing departments to forecast that its products will increase the firm's share of the market. It is not surprising, therefore, to find that an aggregate of the forecasts of the individual competitors in the industry will almost invariably produce a total in excess of 100 per cent.

A forecasting team needs a devil's advocate: that is to say, someone should assess the strength of the competition and its impact on market shares. It is also necessary to have a cautious view of the market as a whole, taking into account the obvious and the less obvious trends in the form of competition between whole sectors of industry for the consumers' spending power. Finally, some allowance should be made for unforeseen shocks which tend to affect the economic scene at an average of some four to five year intervals.

Investment projects

The analysis of investment projects accounts for a major part of a firm's forecasting work. Major investments entail forecasts of both sales and costs. In most cases it will be necessary to incorporate a forecast of interest rates and this may extend to such varied items as raw material costs and the price of land.

The object of the forecasts and analysis is to establish the likely return on capital employed in the project in question and to compare this with the firm's target rate of return. The capital costs of the project will have been determined from quotations for the plant and machinery and other assets to be acquired. Some allowance will also be made for a share of the firm's existing fixed assets, since these will contribute to the functioning of the new investment. In addition, allowance will be made for a share of working capital.

The forecasts of the sales revenue to be generated by a major project may require market research. Some large organizations have their own market research departments, but in most cases surveys will have to be commissioned. The research will generate a range of estimates of the total market and the market share. The forecaster will thus be provided with a marker for the potential size of the project's sales revenue. This estimate must be refined to establish a profile of the build-up of sales and the ultimate rate of growth over the life of the product. In most cases the product will have a defined life. Technical progress and competition will gradually erode the market life of the product as well as the useful life of the asset. The time horizon of the sales forecast is therefore likely to be around ten years, or even less where there is a fast pace of technical change. Conversely, long-lived assets, such as a power station, will require a much longer sales and cost time horizon and the long-run of forecasts revenues will need to be discounted at a rate of interest to establish the discounted cash flow.

The cost forecasts must allow for increases in pay rates as well as changes in prices of materials and components bought in, plus estimates for consumption of energy and services, including transport, insurance, local and national taxes and various other overheads. It will be necessary to forecast changes in numbers employed and the wage and salary bill, including the costs of social security and pension provisions.

This body of forecasting work will flow from the broad forecasts of the national and international economies outlined in Part 1. The sales forecast must be consistent with the forecasts of the sector covering the product generated by the proposed investment and the cost forecasts must also be consistent with the forecast of national pay trends, raw material and service prices.

There will inevitably be a degree of uncertainty in the forecasts and a number of scenarios should be examined to determine the prospective return on capital employed in the project. This exercise may show the return on the project to be below target and unacceptably low. As a result the project should be re-examined and modified. It may be possible to redesign the project so as to reduce the capital cost and also to revise the product mix and sales plan to improve the return.

The forecasting discipline, therefore, can through its flexibility lead to a more certain investment project giving an acceptable rate of return. Where assets are being replaced the forecasts will be largely concerned with the prospective change in operating costs. In nearly every case the new plant and machinery will have a substantially higher productivity and will increase productive capacity. The same output may therefore be achieved with less manpower so that the saving in labour costs will be the major item in establishing the return on capital employed. Since pay rates will almost certainly rise over the life of the replacement assets, labour saving enhances the return on capital employed.

The same logic applies to the replacement of buildings. New factories, warehouses and offices provide the opportunity to improve layout and access, save energy and improve the flow of materials and products, as well as to enhance the environment and working conditions. In some cases changes are imposed by legislation. Health and safety measures may compel firms to make investments and to replace assets without necessarily generating any savings. Nevertheless, there is a case for analysing such projects and attempting to find savings and improved productivity so as to generate a return on capital employed, even if below the firm's target rate of return.

A merger with another business, or a takeover, will also require an investment analysis and a set of forecasts. This will entail an appraisal of both businesses to establish to what extent the firms overlap and the likely economies.

The same method of investment analysis must be made to the forecasting of the target firm's sales and costs. The analysis will be more difficult since the historical records of the target firm may not be available in detail and there may be problems of interpretation arising from accounting methods. The target firm may have had difficulties which have been disguised. It is therefore prudent to make a cautious interpretation of the historical record and the apparent trends.

In framing the forecasts of prospective sales, costs and productivity, allowance should be made for possible hidden problems and the difficulties of melding the two sets of management and personnel. In many cases mergers do not achieve the anticipated results. The buyer's optimism may result in too high a price for the acquisition and there is a tendency to assume that there will be synergy in selling two sets of products which is not attainable.

A balanced approach to management

Much of the emphasis in investment planning and forecasting centres on the use of labour, saving labour and raising productivity. Yet any enterprise, if it is to survive and prosper, has to recognize that it is necessary to satisfy all those people who contribute, in one way or another, to the business in question. This means, in the first place, that the firm must satisfy its customers. In other words, it must provide the kinds of goods and services that its customers need and give them value for money. At the same time, it is essential that the workers at all levels are adequately rewarded and satisfied. Just as the staff must satisfy the firm's customers, so must they endeavour to secure satisfactory levels of pay and conditions of work. By the same token, it is necessary to satisfy the individuals who, through their savings, provide the capital used in the productive process.

In practice, the business cannot succeed if it satisfies only one or even two of these three interests. If one of the parties is not satisfied then the business will fail. Therefore, a successful enterprise has to reconcile the interests of these three sets of people (see Diagram 8.2).

In some countries the legal system lays down that the shareholders' interests are paramount in the running of a business. That is to say, the managers of the business are answerable to the owners and not to the workers and customers. In practice, it has only been possible to satisfy the owners' interests by satisfying workers', managers' and customers' interests alike. This reality has gradually been recognized by the extension of government regulations to control monopolies and many aspects of business affairs. Steps have been taken to protect the consumer and there has been a steady increase in legal obligations to protect employees.

Diagram 8.2   The three partners

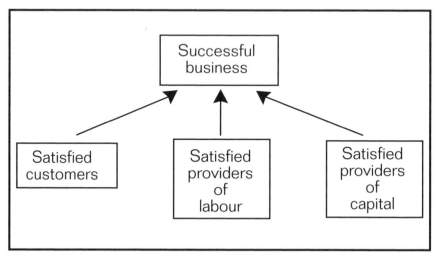

Although the analysis of the way a firm is run does not depend upon a forecast, there are occasions where a forecast of another firm – a competitor or a takeover target – requires a careful study of the way it is run and its strengths and weaknesses. Insufficient concern for customers or staff would be faults which would need to be projected into the forecasts. It is essential to establish the extent to which the two firms would be compatible.

Conclusions

- In setting targets, allowance must be made for future changes in the operating environment.
- The target rate of return on investment must be set in relationship to the forecast levels of interest rates and inflation.
- In formulating a business plan, it is essential to take into account the history of the firm through the previous decade and to identify its strengths and weaknesses and its key operating ratios.
- The efficiency of management can be judged by the return on the total capital employed in the business as distinct from the return on shareholders' funds. The company's subsidiaries and divisions should be assessed in the same way.
- Where the board has set targets for a horizon year the planner must forecast the path of the business cycle year by year through the forecast periods to take account of cyclical variations.
- The firm's plan must be based on a consistent set of assumptions about the future. Those assumptions will shape the forecasts.
- The assumptions must include international and national factors and a range of items covering markets, costs and prices having a direct bearing on the business.
- In many cases businesses will obtain forecasts of national economies from the professional forecasting firms and institutions. Be wary of computerized models since the statistical raw material is often suspect.
- The computerized model is useful for testing the significance of differing assumptions
- Use a Delphi forecasting exercise to draw out a range of plausible scenarios and to test ideas about the firm's future.
- The forecaster must allow for a continuous process of product change and innovation in an industry and allow for competition in predicting market shares.
- Most of a firm's forecasting work is concerned with investment. Large projects may require market research.
- Much of investment planning and forecasting centres on the use of labour and its cost.

Sources

The Power of the Machine (Buchanan).

Preparing for the Twenty-First Century (Kennedy).

The End of Work (Rifkin).

The Long Wave in the World Economy (Tylecot).

National income accounts.

9 COSTS AND PRICES

Although some costs are beyond the firm's control, certain features of costs and selling price are wholly or partly determined by the firm's own decisions. As discussed in previous chapters, costs of energy and commodities are determined by international and national market forces. Interest rate costs and taxation bearing on a business and its customers are inevitably beyond the firm's control.

Yet even where labour costs, for example, are largely determined by national and local market forces a firm can adopt a flexible policy towards pay and incentives that enables it to exercise a fair degree of control over its cost of labour.

Labour costs in the national economy

In the final analysis, virtually all costs can be attributed to labour. Apart from its direct labour bill, when a firm buys in materials and components, energy and services, it is buying other people's labour in an indirect way. Thus, even imports can be thought of as a labour cost – in this case the labour of foreign workers.

Labour costs are estimated by dividing the increase in the labour bill (wages and salaries) by the increase in total output of the economy measured in volume terms. The resultant figure is the change in labour costs per unit of output. Thus, if wages and salaries have risen by 10 per cent and output by 4 per cent, unit labour costs will have risen by 5·8 per cent ($1·10 \div 1·04 = 1·058$).

A firm must estimate its own historical labour costs per unit of output in order to make comparisons with the national record and the labour costs in its own industry. This is a difficult exercise since the firm's output of a range of goods and services may be hard to quantify in volume, or real, terms. A major car manufacturer, for example, will produce a range of vehicles of different sizes and values. To divide the growth in the total wage bill by the change in the total number of vehicles produced may well produce a false estimate of the change in the firm's labour costs. Estimates must therefore be made for the attributable labour costs for each model to establish separate measures of labour cost.

In some cases the physical volume of production is difficult to determine. Many services are sold on a value basis. In banking and retailing, it is impossible to determine the number of units produced. A bank will know the number of cheques it has cleared and the average value of its clearings. The growth in that average can be deflated by the general level of price inflation for the economy as a whole. A notional estimate of the change in the volume of output can be derived in this way. However, that measure takes no account of the changes in its loan portfolio or its bad debts.

In retailing, the change in the firm's sales measured in cash values can be deflated by the change in the national consumer price index to obtain a measure of the firm's turnover, or gross output, measured in real terms. Although crude, this process will make it possible to estimate labour cost per unit of output and this method can be applied to the firm's individual branches and product ranges.

A forecast of the firm's labour costs must start from a forecast of the national labour scene. Although trade union membership and power has tended to lessen in the USA and a number of other industrial economies, unions still play a major role in wage negotiations and settlements. These settlements are generally on a national basis. There is, therefore, a national pattern which will influence other industry and individual firm's pay deals.

The overall demand for labour is the dominant force in determining national pay rates. The level of unemployment and unfilled job vacancies provide a barometer of those forces. Demand will vary from industry to industry and location to location and it is important to remember that employees will have some knowledge of pay rates in the area in which they live. Labour mobility ensures that rates of pay in a town or city will tend to move by a similar rate. The demand for particular skills will be reflected in wage differentials and skill shortages will force pay rates up at an above-average rate.

The calculation of the changes in national labour costs is derived from wage rates, the total wages and salaries bill and the total output of the economy in real terms. The arithmetic is shown in the following hypothetical example using five-year cycles shown in Table 9.1. The wage and salary bill, which includes social security costs, will almost invariably rise faster than wage rates since pay is boosted by overtime payments and bonuses. This difference is known in the jargon as wage drift. The example shows a declining pace of pay increases in a period of relatively high unemployment and job insecurity as a result of cost cutting and accelerating technological change. The average rate of growth in output is assumed to stick at 2·7 per cent per annum. Wage costs per unit of output decelerate to show an increase of 2·0 per cent per annum through the forecast ten-year period.

The exercise implies that output per person employed – labour productivity – accelerates to some extent, reflecting the increases in investment associated with the introduction of new technology.

COSTS AND PRICES • 137

Table 9.1   A forecast of national labour cost (average annual rate of change, %)

	Wage rates	A Wages and salaries	B Total output	A÷B Wage costs per unit of output
1985–90	5.5	6.6	3.0	3.5
1990–95	5.0	5.5	2.3	3.1
1995–00	4.7	5.3	2.7	2.5
2000–05	4.5	5.0	2.7	2.2
2000–10	4.4	4.8	2.7	2.0

Apart from the general pressures of supply and demand in the labour market, employers and employees pay attention to changes in the cost of living as measured by retail prices and the cost of living index. No-one willingly accepts a fall in spending power. Trade unions will seek to achieve pay settlements which are above the rate of price inflation so as to deliver an increase in spending power. However, when profits are under pressure and falling, employees may be willing to accept a pay cut or pay standstill in order to protect jobs.

Where the economy is slowing towards recession more firms are in difficulties and overtime and bonus payments fall. The gap between the rate of change in the total pay bill (wages and salaries) and wage rates narrows and in recession may even reverse, should there be widespread short-time working. In a continental economy, such as the USA, market conditions can differ significantly between regions and pay levels and changes will reflect these differences. The same features will be found in smaller national economies as a result of differences in industrial performance.

Costs in the firm

Although national and local pay levels and trends are key factors in compiling a labour cost forecast for the individual firm, the firm's policies can result in a different pattern of costs. The growth in labour productivity will differ and efficiency in the use of labour is directly under the control of the firm.

Growth industries, where demand is rising at an above-average rate, do not necessarily have a high rate of growth in labour productivity. Where sales are expanding at a good rate, profitability will probably be high and management will not be under pressure. In a declining industry, however, competition will be fierce and firms will be struggling to survive. In these circumstances productivity tends to rise at an above-average rate since management will be forced to reduce costs to maintain, or improve, profit margins. The numbers employed will be reduced, boosting the productivity per person of the remaining labour force.

High productivity can be achieved by using more advanced technology. Automated controls and computerized systems used in robot production lines are operated with the minimum of labour. High productivity can also be achieved by other methods. I was adviser for many years to a firm which operated a shift system so as to ensure 24 hour per day working for seven days a week. Continuous operation was achieved by undemanding technology where there was little chance of machine failure holding up production. Plants were shut down twice a year for maintenance and replacement of machines and, of course, holidays. The effectiveness of the operation was reflected in the high rate of return on capital employed. The firm's employment policy was aimed at preventing the intrusion of trade unions and to maintain continuous production. It therefore paid 10 per cent more than the average of other manufacturing firms in the area and provided a generous pension scheme for all.

The firm has to construct cost and price forecasts of various items in its management accounts. In this form the accounts are an essential part of the forward plans of the business. Every stage of development of a business plan should contain an assessment of costs and financial flows, while financial accounts relating to the plan form the principal and ultimate piece of information on which planning decisions are taken. Standard costs are a simple example of this.

The function of accounting for the future is the same as accounting for the immediate past. It is to assure the owners of the business that their investment is being looked after with skill and probity, and that other functions of the business can operate from a firm financial base. Naturally, the degree of certainty about future accounts is less, since they cannot rest on the secure base of double entry book keeping. Because the future itself is uncertain, probability statements replace actuals.

Forecasting under different accounting systems

The accountancy profession has long been aware of the need for forecasting costs such as wages and specific materials. Equally with capital items, historical accounting systems contain clear rules for simulating future valuations and depreciation. Thus consistency can be attained between past, present and future sets of accounts.

The accountant is responsible for seeing that these forecasts are made available, usually from his normal contacts with operating departments. He may accept what he is given, but more usually his training suggests that an audit from an independent source is desirable. It may be that the operating department is not skilled in forecasting and the accountant is left with the task unaided.

At this stage of the forecasting process, therefore, it is often useful for the accountant to have at his disposal some relevant forecasts prepared by an independent forecasting organization. Based as they are on clearly stated assumptions, such forecasts, whether for costs and prices in the economy as a whole or for individual sectors of labour and material costs, are an integral part of the set of relationships by which consistency is achieved between major elements of the forecasts for the whole economy. In few instances should an individual firm make forecasts of this type: it is wasteful in effort, time and cost for it to attempt to do so.

Costs and prices produced by forecasting institutes can sometimes be used directly without much alteration but should not be used blindly. With labour costs, for example, the percentage change in the national average forecast from year to year may indeed follow closely the labour costs in the firm irrespective of the mix of labour needed. But more broadly, and quite independently of the degree to which the general fits the individual case, such central forecasts are prepared to match a stated set of assumptions. Because any firm is part of the total economy, these assumptions are valuable as a scene setter for the firm's own thinking about its own forecasts. Quite often it is not too much to claim that the benefits of thinking through the assumptions outweigh the benefits gained from the detailed numerical forecasts which follow.

The firm is more usually quite different from the average for the UK. Either the ratio of types of labour within the firm (for example, skilled, semi-skilled, unskilled or salaried management to hourly paid) is individual to it or the firm uses a mix of materials and fuel which is quite different from the national average, with differential effects on its own costs. Again it will be unusual if its proportion of labour to material costs is identical with the national average.

There are three basic methods by which the accountant can make his forecasts with the use of central cost and price forecasts. The first is to attempt to find a relationship between each particular cost to the firm and the same national average. Often a simple chart will suffice, or a more formal relationship established even by unsophisticated statistical techniques. Much will depend upon the availability of historical data, for the relationship in previous business cycles will provide a sound basis for forecasting the course of prices in the next business cycle. The cycles have averaged about five years in length over the period from 1945. For this reason it is essential to have data for the past five years and preferably for ten or more. A relationship based on one business cycle may be inadequate for forecasting. The evidence of two cycles is more convincing and in addition provides a basis for gauging changes in trend from cycle to cycle.

In moving forward from base to forecast, it is essential to think which of the background factors may be changing. Changes in legislation must be considered. When relevant, these items must be incorporated into the forecasts.

The forecast system can be considerably strengthened when a range of costs forms part of a total which can be separately forecast by reference to some national average. The individual forecasts must match with that for the total.

The second method is to select key elements from the national and international factors relating to the base cost or price items to be forecast. In the overall, or aggregate, forecasts these assumptions are themselves dealt with in the round. These special factors can then be analysed individually and applied to an individual base for each cost or price. The virtue of this method is that, having conducted analysis on two different levels, each can be used to check the other.

The third method is to identify the major components of cost which go to make up the total cost or price to be forecast and the relative importance of each in the final price to be forecast. The bought in forecasts for each component can then be used with given statistical weights to form a weighted average for each forecast period.

A national costs and prices model

The professional forecasting institutions use models of factors and relationships which determine costs and prices in the national economy. It is essential to understand the structure of the model if these external forecasts are to be used to help forecast costs and prices for the individual firm.

Diagram 9.1 illustrates the flows and relationships which generate the final cost and price changes. It will be seen that sets of assumptions have first to be made with regard to the world and then the national economy. Assumptions have to be made regarding fiscal policy, which will embrace changes in taxation and government spending, as well as monetary policy and social factors. The fiscal assumptions are critical in that these will imply certain levels of public sector borrowing and this in turn will have a large bearing on the growth of money supply.

Money supply is a crucial factor in determining price changes. It is literally true to say that money makes the world go round. Where there is surplus money it is almost inevitable that the faster growth in money supply will lead to faster growth in spending and ultimately to faster growth in prices. Thus a 5 per cent growth in money supply when consumer prices are rising by 2 per cent leaves a crude money surplus of 3 per cent. That surplus will feed through into higher costs and prices over a period of about two years. The

Diagram 9.1   Costs and prices

Prices

Costs

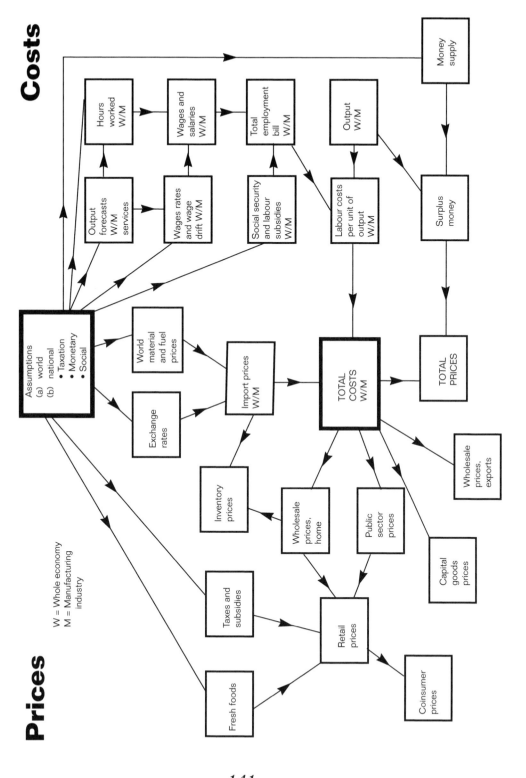

W = Whole economy
M = Manufacturing
industry

diagram shows this as bearing on total prices in the economy, known in the jargon as the GDP deflator.

So far as the social factors are concerned, these will embrace attitudes towards work and pay as well as the pressures which are ultimately reflected in politics and government action.

It is also necessary to take as an assumption the output forecasts for the economy as a whole as well as the split between output in manufacturing industry and in the service industries. These forecasts can then be translated into the number of hours worked in the economy, and the forecast of labour input is derived from estimates of the rate of change in output per man hour.

Labour productivity is measured from the historic trends from one cycle to the next. In broad terms, output per man hour rises at around 2 per cent per annum in the mature economies. Since hours worked tend to decline owing to longer holidays and a shorter working week, output per man year has been on a trend rising at a slightly lower rate.

There is a cyclical fluctuation in the relationship and when output is growing slowly labour productivity also grows at a below-average rate for the reason that employers seldom reduce the overall number of people employed to the same extent, so that the time spent at work does not decline proportionately with the fallback in the rate of output growth. Conversely, when output is rising at an above-average rate labour productivity also rises faster because labour is used more intensively and the slack is taken up.

Fluctuations in the tempo of activity throughout the business cycle also determine the extent of overtime working. Throughout the period from 1945 wage earnings have risen faster than wage rates. What tends to happen is that, in slack times, when there is little overtime working, wage rates and wage earnings tend to rise more or less at the same rate. When output is rising more rapidly, earnings rise faster than wage rates and this gap, as noted above, is known as wage drift. As is shown in the diagram, working from the assumptions and the output forecasts, the forecasts of hours worked are constructed and the forecasts are made both of wage rates and of wage drift. These forecasts can then be married to produce forecasts for the total wage and salary bill.

It will be seen that at each stage the calculations are made both for the economy as a whole and for the manufacturing industry. There is a clear relationship between the two and the forecasts for the economy as a whole are used as a basis for the estimates of the manufacturing industry. The fluctuations in output and pay in manufacturing are greater than for the economy as a whole, so that in the upturn of the cycle manufacturing wages will tend to rise faster than the national average and then drop back to the national average in the slack periods of the cycle. This relationship is established by examining the differences in performance in the previous business cycles.

To move from the total wages and salaries bill to the total employment bill requires a set of assumptions about the changes in social security taxes and labour subsidies. The forecasts must contain assumptions for the year-to-year changes in social security and pension contributions as well as the changes in labour subsidies, such as job-creation schemes. Some important changes are signposted for several years ahead.

We are now in a position to estimate labour costs per unit of output. The separate forecasts of output for the whole economy and for manufacturing industry are then matched with the forecast total employment bill for the two items. The changes in employment bill are divided by the changes in output to arrive at the figure for labour costs per unit of output.

Total wages, salaries and other labour costs account for between 60 and 70 per cent of national income and output in the national economies and as a rule of thumb it can be assumed that labour accounts for close to two-thirds of all costs in the final analysis. This figure is far higher than the labour cost fraction in the average business. The big figure includes the labour costs of making and supplying energy, materials components and services, such as post, telephone and transport. Taken to its extreme, labour costs feature in capital purchases of building, plant and machinery so that virtually all costs have an extremely high labour cost.

As is shown in Diagram 9.1, these forecasts are then fed into the total cost calculations and are married with the forecasts of import prices. This section of the forecasts is of over-riding importance because of labour dominance in the total cost structure of an economy. The method outlined here is relevant to any economy and is the first stage in producing overall cost estimates and, ultimately, price forecasts. What stands out from the outline of the forecasting system is that only a small part of the work can be regarded as mechanical and it will be seen that the end forecasts are no better than the assumptions adopted at the outset. It is for this reason that we stress the importance of political judgement and an awareness of social pressures in reaching agreement on the pattern of assumptions to be adopted for the period to be forecast.

It will also be apparent that there is a great value in adopting alternative sets of assumptions so that forecasts can be constructed to illustrate various outcomes. A sensitivity analysis using this technique will help to give a greater degree of assurance in formulating future policies.

Having completed the labour cost forecasts we now turn to examine the system for forecasting import prices and material costs and then the derivation of prices. Having forecast labour costs per unit of output for the whole economy and manufacturing industry, assumptions and forecasts must be made for the world economy so as to predict the world inflation factor and the prices of UK imports and materials.

From the forecasts of world output estimates are made of the changing levels of demand for materials. Commodity prices fluctuate on average with the world business cycle, with a time lag of up to one year. In the recession phases, when world industrial production is growing slowly, the easing of demand for commodities results in a general weakening of commodity prices. In the upswing of industrial production, after a time lag, commodity prices begin to rise and to accelerate. For most of the period from 1945 commodity prices fell when world industrial production rose at less than 5 per cent per annum and accelerated when the industrial growth rate was above 5 per cent per annum. The relationship has weakened to some extent but the principle still holds. From the forecasts of world output growth separate forecasts are derived for world commodity prices and national import costs.

In parallel with these forecasts separate forecasts are made of exchange rate movements. The key determinant of these movements is the relative movement of prices country by country, as discussed in Chapter 3. The relative inflation rates in fact influence exchange rates and, using the range of forecasts, it is possible to establish the average exchange rate movements for the currency in question.

The forecasts of world prices are then married with the exchange rate forecast to produce a set of import price forecasts for the national economy in question. These, in turn, are used to construct separate forecasts of import prices for the manufacturing industry. The forecasts of import prices as a whole, both for goods and services, and also the import price forecasts for the manufacturing industry, are then married with unit labour cost forecasts for the two sectors. It is now possible to determine the forecasts of total prices in the economy as a whole (the GDP deflator) using the cross-checks.

There is a time lag between the changes in total costs in the economy and total prices of up to three-quarters. This lag is readily understood if it is remembered that the movement of materials from imports through the warehouse into the factory, through work-in-progress to finished goods, to the wholesaler and finally to the retailer, is a lengthy process, and the average of stocks held in the country may amount to over half a year's total output. It is thus logical that the time lag from costs through to final prices is as long as nine months.

Matching these two forecasts for total prices gives a base for constructing other prices in the economy which must in aggregate produce the same overall deflator.

With these separate estimates of total cost movements for the whole economy and the manufacturing industry, we can now proceed to construct separate price forecasts. The most important of these is the series for wholesale prices of manufactures to the home market. Taking the two ingredients of price costs in manufacturing, there is a time lag between changes in labour costs and selling prices of between three and six months. The lag between imports and material costs and selling prices is between six and nine months. The total cost effect takes as long as two years to work right through the economy, though most of the impact will have taken place in six months to a year.

Wholesale prices of manufactures to the home market will also determine changes in inventory prices. In forecasting the movements in stock prices, wholesale prices and import prices are married together.

Turning to the construction of the forecasts of retail prices, separate forecasts are also required for taxes and subsidies and for fresh food prices, as well as for the utilities, which in many countries are publicly owned. Separate assumptions are required for these items. Taxes and subsidies are changed through the budgets from year to year and these assumptions must conform with the overall assumptions about fiscal policy. Public sector prices may also be the result of political decisions, so that assumptions are necessary about the rate of change in those prices.

Fresh food prices are subject to changes in supply and demand brought about by climatic conditions and to this extent these are unpredictable over the longer-term. However, for the immediate present and the year ahead a known shortage can confidently be assumed to result in above-average price rises. These factors must then be incorporated into the overall forecasts of the retail prices. The four sets of forecasts are married to produce estimates for movements of an index of retail or consumer prices. This is the most widely used price index in the economy and has a great bearing on wage and income determination.

A distinction must be made between a price index constructed for a fixed list of goods and services and an index covering consumers' spending as a whole. The latter will be derived from the national income accounts where each category of spending is valued in both current prices and real terms. The grand totals in current prices and real terms provide the basis for measuring consumer price changes for the whole range of spending. Thus the consumer price deflator, obtained by calculating the changes in spending in current prices by the changes in the series in real terms, will yield an index of consumer prices, known as the consumer price deflator.

As shown in Diagram 9.1, the major components of retail prices are forecast separately and from this base a forecast of consumer prices as a whole is derived. As a general rule a retail price index based on monthly samples of prices tends to overstate the rate of price inflation since consumers change their pattern of spending in response to price changes. In seeking best value, needs are often met by finding cheaper alternatives.

The forecasts of consumers' prices (the consumer price deflator) are incorporated in the overall forecasts for the economy and, because consumers' spending is by far the largest item of demand, this price factor has the greater significance in the overall forecasts.

From the general forecasts for the whole economy and the manufacturing industry's costs, separate forecasts are made for the prices of capital goods with separate indices for plant and machinery. Some guidance can be gained from these estimates as to future replacement costs and the determination of depreciation provisions. Export prices are also determined from the total cost forecasts for the manufacturing industry and in this case the world inflation forecasts and exchange rate forecasts are used to obtain the estimates of export prices.

It will be seen that the forecasting model for costs and prices provides a network of data for use in business management and planning. Market policies will be more confidently determined given a set of inflation forecasts. Business financing and cash flow will also be forecast with a much greater appreciation of cyclical changes and risk when using cost and price forecasts of this nature.

Seasonal adjustment

Much of the data used in business analysis and forecasting is derived from monthly surveys. The national series are generally presented in a seasonally adjusted form as well as the unadjusted form.

In many cases sales and prices vary from season to season through the year. In those countries where Christmas is celebrated retail sales in December are around twice as high as the monthly average. Production to meet Christmas demand is therefore above average in the months before December. It then drops and retail sales in February are usually the lowest of the year.

Similarly, food prices vary through the year with the crop seasons. When fresh fruit and vegetables come into the markets prices are generally lower. Those items will be imported at other times, so that in the richer economies supplies are available from all parts of the world the year round. Even so, food prices fluctuate with a seasonal pattern which is distorted from time to time by both shortages and gluts. Abnormal weather may damage crops or interrupt supplies, forcing prices up, whilst abundant crops will depress prices, in some cases to the point where it is not worth the farmer's while to harvest them.

To establish the underlying trends in both sales and prices it is necessary to apply seasonal corrections to the monthly figures. The great majority of series display a seasonal pattern and this is easily illustrated by plotting the monthly figures on a chart over a run of years. The average seasonal fluctuations are calculated by constructing moving 12-month averages. The monthly figures for a year are averaged and then the February to January figures, the March to February figures and so on. The averages should be completed for a run of five or more years. It is then possible to compare the actual monthly figures with those for the moving averages, which indicate the seasonally adjusted trend. The divergence from trend for each January, February, March and so on can now be averaged and expressed as a percentage, giving a tool for applying a seasonal correction for each new set of monthly figures.

The firm must apply this technique to its own figures in order to derive a trend. That trend will almost certainly display a cyclical movement over the years. For forecasting purposes the trends in a firm's sales, prices paid for supplies and its own selling prices can then be applied to the trends in the seasonally adjusted national series. In this connection it is vital for the firm to maintain a diary in which the unusual events which have affected the business are recorded. Features which disrupt supplies or sales, such as abnormal weather, strikes or political disturbances should be logged. The diary should be referred to when making an analysis of the past record as part of a forecast. These unusual events are often forgotten or overlooked and in many cases the data are not treated with the reverence they deserve and in some cases are destroyed. Since staff turnover tends to be above average in sales and marketing departments, the chances are that the personnel do not have the intimate knowledge of the firm's sales record. Hence the importance of a diary.

Conclusions

- All costs, except land, originate directly or indirectly from labour.
- There is a national pattern of pay settlements which influences settlements in other industries and individual firms.
- The level of unemployment and unfilled job vacancies provide a barometer of demand for labour and changes in pay rates.
- Local conditions in cities and towns also determine pay levels in the area.
- Changes in the cost of living, measured by retail or consumer price indices, influence both employees and employers in wage bargaining.
- Labour productivity, directly under the firm's control, tends to rise faster in declining industries where firms struggle to survive.
- Productivity can be enhanced not only by new technology but by combinations of profit sharing and bonus schemes and enlightened labour management.
- Most firms will find it helpful to use forecasts prepared by an independent forecasting organization.
- Money supply is a crucial factor in determining price changes over a period of around two years.
- In the mature economies output per man hour rises at around 2 per cent per annum.

- Forecasts are no better than the assumptions on which they are based. Political judgement and awareness of social pressures are particularly important.
- There is a time lag of up to three-quarters between the changes in total costs in the economy and total prices.
- It is necessary to apply seasonal corrections to the firm's monthly sales, costs and prices to establish the underlying trends.
- It is vital for the firm to maintain a diary as a reminder of events which have had an abnormal effect on business.

Sources

'Main Economic Indicators' (OECD, monthly).

Seasonal Patterns in Business and Everyday Life (Thorneycroft).

Forecasting for Business (Wood and Fildes).

Business Forecasting: An Economic Approach (Robinson).

National income accounts.
Cost and price series from international and national sources.
International financial statistics (IMF, monthly and annually).

10 FORECASTING FROM A MODEL OF THE BUSINESS

The financial records of a business contain all the data describing its history and its progress. In short, the records show how the business works. It follows, therefore, that the construction of a model from the firm's financial history provides a platform for building a set of forecasts outlining that firm's future.

A business employs labour and capital to produce goods and services. It buys materials, energy and a range of services to make its products. It adds value to those purchases via its labour force and capital in making the things it sells. The difference between the firm's sales revenue and what it buys to produce those sales is added value.

Value added

A firm's first objective is to create added value. That surplus is divided between labour and gross profits (pre-interest, depreciation and tax) so that an objective to maximize profits first requires the creation of added value.

Although only a minority of public companies report value added in their accounts, it is possible to estimate it from the accounts since, in addition to reported profits, firms are obliged to state what was paid to labour (including pension contributions) and in some cases the number of employees. Thus, by adding employees' remuneration and gross profits, it is possible to estimate the firm's value added for the year.

Value added is an attractive measure of performance since it is not complicated by taxation, or by accounting conventions. It is quite unambiguous and from three simple factors a range of useful yardsticks can be derived for comparing performance. These are (a) value added (split between labour and profits), (b) capital employed (on a current cost basis, derived from insurance valuations), and (c) numbers employed. From the three factors we can derive the following:

- value added/net capital employed;
- value added per employee;
- value added per monetary unit (dollar, sterling and so on) of pay;
- net capital employed per employee;

- employees' share of value added;
- profits' share of value added;
- changes in employment;
- the change in value added per employee (equals labour productivity); and
- the split between home and foreign activity.

Diagram 10.1 shows how value added is derived and how it is allocated. The lion's share is absorbed by labour costs. The residue (gross profit) has to provide for depreciation provisions, interest costs, taxation, dividends and profits retained to help finance future development. As an example, the value added allocation for the companies included in the *Financial Times* Actuaries 100 Share Index as at August 1986 is shown in Table 10.1. Value added amounted to nearly a third of sales revenue. Labour's share was just over a

Diagram 10.1 The split of revenue and value added

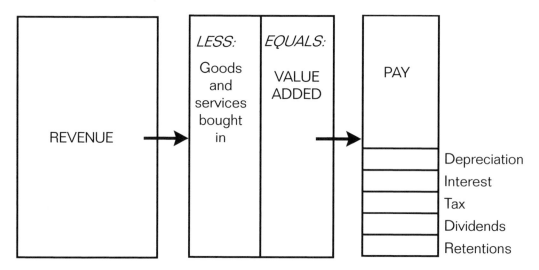

Table 10.1 Value added and its allocation for the FTA 100 Share Index companies as at August 1986

			%
Sales revenue			100
less bought-in goods and services			68
equals value added			32
of which:	earned in the UK	(55)	18}
	earned abroad	(45)	14}
	labour's share	(52)	17}
	gross profit share	(48)	15}
of which:	retentions		6

half and 40 per cent of the gross profit share was retained and ploughed back into the firm, accounting for 6 per cent of value added.

In that year the value added of the 100 companies was equivalent to 22 per cent of UK gross domestic product. The numbers employed by the companies accounted for 13 per cent of national employment whilst the market capitalization of the 100 was 71 per cent of the All Share Index total. The 100 share index sample, however, was by no means typical of the 'average' British company.

The same analysis, completed in 1989 for the 100 company sample, covering annual results for the five years with year ends in 1988, is shown in Table 10.2. Retained cash flow is the sum of retained profits and the depreciation provision. The annual average rate of change over the five-year period shows sales revenue rising faster than purchases. As a result value added grew at a faster pace. Similarly, the share of gross profits in value added grew faster than labour's share. Retained cash flow rose more rapidly, at nearly 18 per cent per annum.

Table 10.2   The 100 company summary table performance indices, July 1989

Change on previous year	1983	1988	1983–8 (% p.a.)
Turnover	£202·1bn	£304·3bn	8·5
less purchases	£146·9bn	£211·3bn	7·5
Equals value added	£ 55·2bn	£ 93·0bn	11·0
of which:			
labour's share	£ 34·0bn	£ 49·7bn	7·9
profits' share	£ 21·2bn	£ 43·3bn	15·3
Retained cash flow	£ 9·7bn	£ 22·1bn	17·8
No. of employees[1]	3·99mn	4·39mn	1·9
Value added per employee[2]	£13,835	£21,185	8·9
Retained cash flow per employee	£ 2,440	£ 5,026	15·5
Profits per employee	£ 5,326	£ 9,875	13·1
Ploughback rate[3]			*averages*
	17·6%	23·7%	20·7
Labour's share of value added	61·6%	53·4%	57·5
Profits' share of value added	38·4%	46·6%	42·5

[1] On a full-time equivalent basis; i.e. two part-time = one full-time.
[2] Labour productivity.
[3] Retained cash flow as % of value added figures rounded to nearest decimal point.

Value added per employee expanded by nearly 9 per cent per annum, compared with 13·1 per cent for profits per employee. The rate of price inflation averaged 4·7 per cent through the five-year period. Thus labour productivity improved by 4 per cent per annum in real terms.

The ploughback rate – retained cash flow as a percentage of value added - rose from 17·6 to 23·7 per cent and averaged 20·7 per cent through the period. That addition to capital resources had the potential to raise future value added by around 10 per cent per annum since at that time value added for the 100 companies was equivalent to just over 50 per cent of capital employed.

Whereas two units of capital generated one unit of value added in that sample of companies, four units were required in the economy as a whole. That figure takes account of the social capital employed in the economy covering health, education, transport, utilities, housing and public buildings.

The analysis of the generation and use of a firm's value added throws up a range of historical operating ratios which provide an excellent starting point for projecting its performance into the future. Those ratios reflect embedded trends and for planning and forecasting purposes the first question has to be, 'What will make those ratios change?'

There may be factors in the external environment, discussed in previous chapters, which make an impact on the firm's performance and these should be incorporated into the sales, cost and value added ratios. If, for example, those changes are likely to have an adverse effect on the business performance it will be necessary to work out ways in which performance can be raised to meet the firm's long-term objectives. This will inevitably require new investment to enhance the product as well as investment to improve labour productivity and to reduce costs.

Constructing a model

The analysis of value added must now be extended into a wider set of operating ratios. Whilst value added encapsulates the concept of wealth creation in a simple form, the relationship between value added and capital requires a careful appraisal of the measurement of capital and the accounting conventions.

In this instance we are concerned with the development of a model for a single firm where all the historical material is available. The firm will also have data for its subsidiary companies and operating divisions. It is not possible, however, to build a comprehensive model of other businesses since all that will be available to other companies will be the published company accounts. Whilst value added can be calculated from a set of accounts, there will be no detail of matching information for its subsidiaries and divisions.

Diagram 10.2 Operating ratios

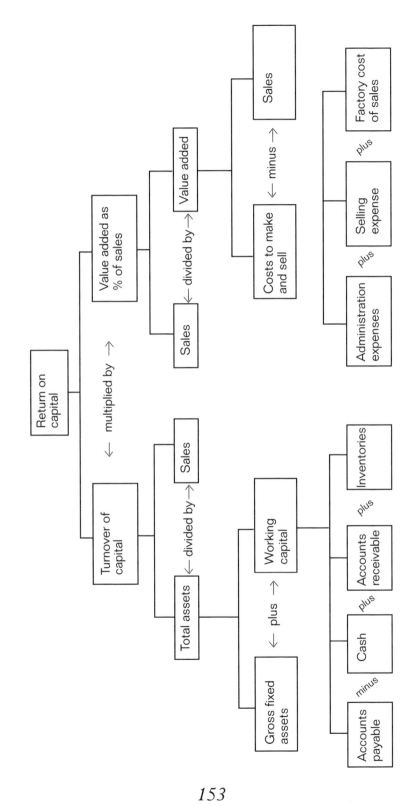

Diagram 10.2 sets out the pattern of operating ratios showing the composition of assets in the total capital employed and the composition of costs in the generation of value added. The ratio of the two aggregates provides a measure of the return of gross profits to total capital employed. The analysis must be extended into greater detail to calculate the return on shareholders' funds and earnings per share.

Once again it is necessary to set out the various factors and ratios year by year – preferably over two cycles – to establish the trends. This body of information describes how the company works. Its strong points and weaknesses are identified and the various solutions to problems can be tested on the model. The data lend themselves to computerization and the analyst can change a ratio to test the effects of that change on other ratios in the model.

In analysing the company's record it is essential, as we have said before, to refer to the company's diary for the period so that due account can be taken of exceptional factors which may have affected performance. These may be national or international features, or specific events bearing on the business, such as a strike in a supplier company disrupting production.

The development of a model of the business can be highly enlightening to the firm's management. Most managers will be familiar with some aspects of the firm's operating ratios. It is unlikely that any one individual will have complete knowledge of the firm's workings. It is unusual for a firm to develop a comprehensive model of itself. Companies confronted by a monopolies investigation may find it necessary to establish a detailed model in an attempt to justify their position. Equally, a takeover battle may force a defender along this route to demonstrate that it is worth much more than the bidder is offering.

The exercise is highly rewarding and, once the model has been constructed, it can be used from year to year to test various courses of action to improve performance. The areas where action may be indicated are as follows:

Using the business model

Sales	• product mix, pricing policy, product development
Purchases	• buy more efficiently, for example using the Internet
	• use materials more efficiently, reducing waste
	• improve deliveries and reduce stockholding
Labour	• improve training and communications
	• motivate involvement in improving productivity
	• consider relating pay, bonuses or profit sharing to value added performance
	• plan manpower and skill requirements
	• improve use of time, skill and energy

Capital
- increase capital intensity
- increase capacity, replacing and updating plant
- improve layout and the flow of production.

Changes in any of these areas will have an impact on other areas, with implications for costs and profitability. Many changes entail capital spending. Investment projects must then be analysed in relation to the associated changes in sales, costs, cash flow and profits.

The kind of detail which can be abstracted from a model is extremely wide. The following list is not exhaustive but covers the salient features needed for effective forecasting and planning.

Use of purchases

- materials/sales
- services/sales

Capital intensity

- assets/employee
- assets/pay
- capital/pay

Use of labour

- value added/pay
- value added/employee
- sales/employee
- pay/employee
- profit/employee
- productivity

Use of capital

- sales/capital
- sales/net assets
- sales/fixed assets
- value added/capital
- stocks/sales
- debtor days
- creditor days

Profitability

- profit/sales
- profit/capital
- profit/net assets
- profit/value added

Financial ratios

- interest cover
- capital leverage
- debt/equity
- cash flow/value added
- earnings per share
- return on shareholders' funds

Reliability of data

A further advantage of the business model is that the company will be in possession of accurate data. Its record of revenue, costs and capital transactions will be exact. As with all businesses, however, the valuation of inventories may be less precise. The board may have laid down precise measures for stocktaking and valuation, endorsed by the firm's auditors. Nevertheless, there are occasions when the value of certain items of stock is a matter of judgement and such judgements may vary over the years.

Another sector which requires careful treatment is the valuation of assets. The firm will have a register of fixed assets showing the purchase price and the accumulated depreciation of the asset. The written-down value is not an accurate representation of the true value of the asset. In market terms an asset can be valued by what it earns or can be made to earn. But this is a matter of guesswork. The more dependable route is to obtain the replacement cost of the asset from the insurance valuations. Using these figures the efficiency of the management can then be judged from calculating the return on capital employed as measured by replacement cost. The use of that method ensures consistency.

In translating the annual report and accounts, care must be taken with the treatment of 'exceptional' items of profit or loss. There are frequently exceptional items to be taken into account and the analyst must make a judgement as to whether the profit should be measured before or after the exceptional adjustment. In most cases the exceptional item should be disregarded in establishing the cyclical trend of the company's profits.

Yet another trap is the treatment of good will resulting from acquisitions of other businesses. In some countries, good will is written off immediately, making a significant dent in the profit trend and the balance sheet. For purposes of analysis it may be more prudent to write off good will over a period of years as if it had a finite life to be accounted for by annual instalments of depreciation.

Whatever the limitations of business accounting, the data provided by the audited accounts are far superior to much of the available national economic data. Some features, such as market prices, interest rates, exchange rates, commodity prices and share prices, can be regarded as hard facts. Most price and pay indices, based on large, regular samples, are fairly accurate. But estimates of spending, saving, profits and capital movements can have dangerous levels of sampling error.

Items of larger, regular spending are captured with a high degree of accuracy by the household spending surveys. These can often be cross-checked from industry data for production and international trade. Similarly the returns for duties, sales and value added taxes provide another cross-check on spending estimates. Thus data covering oil products, alcohol and tobacco are generally dependable.

The smaller the market, the less dependable the survey results. In addition, where households record their spending over a period as part of a survey, the act of recording leads in some cases to a change in the pattern of spending and to underrecording. Spending on such items as drink, tobacco, confectionery, drugs or sex will not be accurately recorded.

The most hazardous areas in national accounting are in the estimation of company and business activity and profits. A company will typically publish its annual accounts around three months after its year end. This means that, where government departments collect business data, whether on a quarterly or an annual basis, the figures relate to a period many months previously. Moreover, companies do not have identical accounting periods and it is difficult to meld together profit data from different periods.

Where a company operates in a number of different industries it may be difficult to abstract data on an industrial basis from the published accounts. Unless the company in question is included in a national survey of industrial production, the relevant data may never be included in the national totals.

Analysis is also made more complex because of the growing number of international corporations. Although turnover may be given in the accounts for operations in different countries, the profits derived from those foreign operations may be distorted by differential pricing of supplies between those businesses.

The movement of capital between companies within an international group may be significant. International capital flows are of vast proportions and, although highly important to the analysis of exchange rate movements and national balance of payments accounting, it is virtually impossible for the national statisticians to track and record those flows within acceptable margins of error.

Relating to the national economy

Although some features of the national economy data are unreliable and subject to major revisions, the forecaster should relate various items from the company's model to matching items in the national economy. The net output of the firm, for example, relates to the gross domestic product. Both items are in fact value added and, where the firm's growth rate has been higher than the national growth rate, it can fairly safely be assumed that this relationship will continue. The firm may, of course, be undergoing a major change, perhaps as a result of more intense competition. In such a case the previous relationship to GDP is unlikely to hold.

The forecaster should use the data for the national economy which are incorporated in its forecasts for the business environment. These will include not only net output forecasts – value added – but a range of cost and price forecasts which will be relevant to cost and price forecasts for the firm. The historical changes in national wage rates, earnings and labour costs should be compared with the firm's historical labour cost changes. Those historical relationships can be applied to the forecasts of national labour costs to derive useful projections for the firm's labour costs.

The establishment of a model of the business is therefore an invaluable means of constructing more confident forecasts and plans. The model, being based on reliable data, provides a means of testing the impact of policy changes and decisions. These can be tested step by step as a piece of sensitivity analysis. This technique helps to minimize risk and brings greater assurance to forecasting, planning and decision taking.

Conclusions

- A firm's financial records show how the business works. Its operating ratios provide a guide to its future.
- A firm's first objective is to create added value. Value added is a simple measure of performance since it is not complicated by taxation and accounting conventions.
- In most cases the largest share of value added is absorbed by labour costs. The improvement in profitability depends to a large extent on raising labour productivity.
- Another critical factor is the ratio of retained cash flow to value added and to capital employed – the ploughback rate. The higher the ploughback rate, the bigger the growth potential.
- The firm's operating ratios, taken back over two cycles, reflect the embedded trends. These provide a starting point for planning and forecasting.
- Value added encapsulates the concept of wealth creation. It is possible to construct a model of the way the firm operates, incorporating ratios related to value added, capital employed and other accounting features.
- The data lend themselves to computerization, enabling the forecaster to test 'what if' assumptions. The effects of a change in one key ratio can then be traced to other ratios, helping to shape planning and investment decisions.
- The firm can use the model to analyse the performance of its subsidiary companies and operating divisions.
- It is essential to maintain a diary so that exceptional events and their effect on past performance can be identified.
- The data available from audited accounts are far superior to much of the available national economic data.
- Allowing for the varying reliability of national statistics, the forecaster should relate some of its key ratios to parallel ratios for the national economy.
- Whereas a firm has all the data and knowledge to build a model of itself, this is not possible for other businesses where the published annual accounts are the only sources available.

Sources

Accountancy manuals for the formulation and interpretation of management accounts and statutory accounts.

National income accounts.

11 FORECASTING PROFITS

In the long run, share prices move in line with profits and earnings per share. The rate of change is frequently out of step, but the timing of stock market changes in direction is closely allied to the turning points in the profits cycle. Over a period of ten years or more the two series will often diverge for a number of years, but in the long run the share price level will reflect the underlying development of corporate profits fairly closely.

Although external factors bearing on profits, such as interest rates, are beyond the firm's control, the management will focus attention on sales, costs and investment with the object of optimizing profits and the company's share price. The aggregation of company profits into a figure for the company sector as a whole provides a measure and a benchmark for judging an individual company's performance which will also be useful in assessing share prices.

It is of the greatest importance to have estimates of profits and cash flow, since the timing of changes in profits is critical so far as management decisions are concerned. Similarly, the connection between share prices and the profit cycle underscores the need to have reliable forecasts of profits for the company sector as a whole as an indicator of likely turning points for the stock market.

A study of the general trends in profits in the economy as a whole provides the firm with a check on the sales and cost forecasts used within the company. A comparison of the general profit trends with the forecasts of the company's profits will focus attention on the assumptions used in the forecasts. There may be special factors working either for or against the firm of particular relevance to cost and price trends and changes in market share.

Profits at the national level

As discussed in Chapter 7, there is considerable difficulty in constructing estimates of company profits earned in a national economy from an analysis of company accounts. This arises from the complexity of international operations and the need to separate profits earned in subsidiaries in other countries. There is a further difficulty in melding together data from a host of companies which do not have a common accounting year.

For these reasons it is advisable to use the national income accounts as the source for compiling a set of forecasts of the company profits sector. The national accounts contain a factor incomes table. The total national income is measured in three ways and, given perfectly accurate measurement, the three methods give the same result. Thus the measure derived from the value of output equals the value of spending and also the value of incomes – as set out in Chapter 1. The reconciliation of the three measures gives a fairly dependable total of national income.

Using this as a starting point, gross profits can be derived by subtracting employment incomes from the total, as shown below:

Total national income, before allowing for depreciation
   and stock appreciation
less: income from employment and self-employment
less: rent
_____
equals: gross trading profits before tax

Forecasts of employment incomes are a component of most forecasts since this is an essential figure in forecasting spending. Employment incomes can be estimated with some confidence, so that subtracting this item from the incomes total, as well as rent, throws up a figure for profits as a residual. Rent is a relatively small item in the accounts.

The profits total will include the surpluses of publicly owned enterprises and, since estimates of this item are shown in the government's budget accounts, the profits total can be divided into the public and private company sectors.

The company profits series will show a clear cyclical pattern and this provides some guidance in identifying turning points not only for profits but for share prices. The two series tend to move together. The significance of this relationship can be attributed to the fact that the profit series is probably a reflection of the overall monetary developments within the economy. Thus, in the upswing of the business cycle, the money supply will be expanding and the economy will become more liquid. Since the company sector tends to lead in the business cycle and to benefit from early gains in the cyclical pattern of productivity, the evident upswing in profits can be seen as a beneficiary of the easing of monetary policy.

The key factor to be kept in mind is that profits are essentially a residual between sales revenue and costs. Since the profit margin is a residual, it follows that relatively small deviations in either the sales series or the costs series can produce marked swings in profits. This is very well understood in business. Having this in mind, it is possible to obtain a cross-check on a profit forecast by adopting two different approaches. In the first case, profits can be estimated as a residual between forecasts of sales revenue and forecasts of costs. Secondly, profits of the company sector can be estimated from their relationship to movements in the economy as a whole. Since profits have a pronounced cyclical pattern, and this pattern can be related to the business cycle in the economy at large, any forecasts of the cycles for the economy should facilitate a forecast of the cycle of profits.

In constructing the profits forecast from sales and costs, sales can be estimated as the product of changes in the volume of output and changes in selling prices. Costs are a sum of two products, namely the volume and price of materials and energy consumed, and wage and salary rates and the amount of labour input. Fluctuations in these factors originate as follows: (a) home demand determines the level of output, (b) the level of output determines the demand for labour, and (c) the demand for labour determines the level of wages. Import prices, on the other hand, must be thought of as external factors determined in world markets.

The internal factors account for some 70 to 80 per cent of all costs of total output in most economies and this large element of costs is influenced by government policy. Labour accounts for the largest part of internal costs. The value added to raw materials in the process of conversion to finished products can be thought of as labour costs incurred at every stage of production and distribution. Thus, although purchases of materials, products and energy from other businesses may account for more than half of total costs, as shown in the company's accounts, in the final analysis it will be seen that supplies bought from other business units will already contain an element for labour cost. Therefore, in an analysis of the economy and the company sector as a whole, guidance can be obtained as to cost movements by paying particular attention to the development of wage rates.

An estimate of sales revenue for the industrial sector can be derived from the series of figures for industrial production (which are available month by month) and the series of wholesale prices of manufactured products. Taking a common base period for both series, an index of sales revenue can be constructed by multiplying the index numbers for production and selling prices.

The exercise for estimating movements in prime costs takes much the same form. Unit labour costs for the industrial sector can be estimated by taking the percentage change in an index of the total wage and salary bill for industry and dividing it by the change in an index of the output of industry. The resultant index indicates changes in the costs of labour per unit of output. Another series is available for the wholesale prices of material and fuel used by the industrial sector. Some estimate has to be made of the proportions of labour and material and fuel used in total output. Guidance as to these proportions is obtainable from the estimates of input and output given in the national income accounts.

In some countries the national accounts include an input/output analysis for the sectors of the economy by industries. The breakdown between major components of costs is sufficiently accurate to indicate the weights to be given to the elements of prime costs in the forecasts. These weights can be applied to labour costs and material costs.

The changes in sales revenue for the industrial sector can now be compared with the changes in prime costs. From this it can be seen how far the movements in profit margins correspond to the business cycle.

The production and cost data are published some months in arrears, so that even if the latest figures for industrial production were reliable – which they are not – the resultant estimate would only indicate the position so far as industrial profit margins were concerned some four months previously. For most purposes of analysis, this is not good enough. Yet, given a long enough run of historical data, it is possible to fit this series into the forecasting model for the economy and to derive estimates, not only of where profits are at any current moment, but for the future period of the forecast.

The relationship between the company sector and the economy as a whole can also be examined from the national income data, in which the product of the company sector and major cost items can be compared with the corresponding data for the whole economy. Having established the cyclical relationships between these series, company profits can now be forecast as part of the national income accounts.

From all the data marshalled for movements in costs and prices and the cyclical relationships between company costs and costs for the whole economy, estimates can be derived of profit movements. Although the resultant series is a forecast of the grand total of profits before depreciation and earned solely in the domestic economy, it still has considerable relevance for industrial sector analysis.

The exercise can be taken forward a great deal further. For the purposes of stock market analysis, estimates of profits earned abroad can be brought in and a notional company account reconstructed by deducting estimates for depreciation and for interest. An illustration of this step is shown below:

Gross trading profits
plus: rent and non-trading income
plus: income from abroad
less: capital consumption (not depreciation)
less: interest
equals: pre-tax profits
      tax ratio %
less: tax accruing
equals: company earnings
      earnings per share adjusted for issues

The figures for earnings per share have to be adjusted to take account of any share issues made during the period in question. These may be stock splits (bonus issues) or rights issues.

Once the analysis has been completed in this way as part of an overall model for the economy, it will be seen that the forecasts can be applied equally well for purposes of stock market analysis, as well as analysis and forecasting of individual companies. In this respect, forecasters in both industry and finance are concerned with the same problems. In the last resort the overriding consideration is to gauge the timing and magnitude of changes in cash flow. Cash flow will be the major consideration in a great number of decisions within the firm. It is also the consideration of the utmost importance to the financial analyst concerned with stock market movements.

Forecasting the individual company's profits

The individual company needs to analyse its own operating ratios and performance for a number of reasons. It is essential that the company should know as much about itself as possible in order to formulate its plans for future development and expansion and to maintain or increase its profitability. Apart from its internal requirements, a company will need to adopt the same methods of analysis in order to study the performance of its rivals and to evaluate other companies for the purposes of mergers and acquisitions.

The disciplines which the company needs to adopt are precisely those which the security analyst will employ in assessing the performance of a whole range of companies from the point of view of portfolio investment. In other words, the security analyst is occupied with the same techniques and objectives as the company planner. Both sets of analysis and forecasts have this in common, namely, that return on capital and prospective earnings per share are the key yardsticks on which they will concentrate.

One of the first steps in analysis is to measure the efficiency of management in relation to return on capital. The management of capital can only be judged in terms of the return achieved on that capital. The results of earlier decisions and day-to-day management are ultimately reflected in profits and the return on capital is probably the most dependable measure we have of the success of management. Thus, for the company to decide upon a target return on capital and a certain prospective level of earnings per share, it will be necessary for past performance and return on capital to be analysed with some care. Similarly, the security analyst will need to pay considerable attention to rates of return on capital achieved in the past and to identifying the reasons for apparent success or failure.

It is important to distinguish between return on capital as a whole and return on assets from the point of view of the shareholder. In order to judge the efficiency of management it is necessary to examine the return obtained on the total stock of assets. How those assets are financed is immaterial. For example, where targets need to be set within a company for its various operating divisions, it will be essential to distinguish the assets under the control of each division and to ask the management of each division to be judged according to the return achieved on those assets. From the point of view of internal control and comparisons it is necessary to have estimates of the gross return on gross assets. Similarly, in order to make comparisons between firms, either within one industry or within the economy as a whole, it is still important to measure the respective efficiency in the use of assets.

The concept of the gross return on gross assets can be thought of as the economic yardstick. Since the analyst is concerned primarily with the question of efficiency in the management of assets, the return measured after depreciation and before tax on the total body of assets, with fixed assets valued at replacement cost, will give the kind of yardstick required for inter-firm comparison and also for comparison within the firm.

Although for purposes of economic assessment it is irrelevant how assets have been financed, it is still essential to analyse the development of the return on shareholders' funds and to set targets in terms of earnings per share. Growth in the return on shareholders' net assets is the most important single factor leading to growth in the share price. The maximization of earnings per share for shareholders will be the prime consideration both of the company and of the security analyst.

The important distinction between the different measures of return is that the return on total capital is a key indicator so far as judging the efficiency of industrial management is concerned, whereas the net return on shareholders' funds is the key indicator in assessing management effectiveness in the interests of shareholders. The second indicator will be dependent upon the first, but the whole question of financing and leverage (gearing) is a subject for separate analysis. Within the company the managers of individual divisions should be concerned with maximizing the return on total assets. The question of maximizing this return in terms of rewards for shareholders is the problem of the board and principally of the finance director. The finance department, or division, must have the responsibility for deciding how assets are to be financed. Risk analysis and financial analysis belong at the centre of the corporation rather than with the divisional management. It is the board's central responsibility to determine the targets for return on equity.

Valuation of assets

As has been emphasized, for the purposes of company analysis it is essential to analyse efficiency in terms of the use of capital. However, there are serious problems in deciding on the basis of assessment. For example, it is no easy matter to measure the value of assets. Ideally, the price of an asset can be defined as the price a buyer will pay for a future stream of income. In this sense the value of an asset will be determined by what that asset will earn. Yet we know in practice that badly used assets, that is to say assets on which a low return is being achieved, will be reflected in a high asset value per share in relation to the share price. The converse will also apply.

Where asset value per share is relatively high, there is some indication of scope for improvement in return on assets through better management. This will not be true in all cases, for it is quite conceivable that return on assets may turn out to be below average, or declining, because of wrong geographical location. The economic decline of an area, or the transfer of an important industry from one region to another, can lead to certain forms of existing investment becoming uneconomic. Changes in taste and fashion can result in an asset becoming obsolete or redundant early in its working life.

For the most part, asset values are measured in terms of balance sheet figures. Companies show fixed assets at original cost less accumulated depreciation. Since replacement prices have risen almost continuously since the 1930s, such a basis of valuation is unrealistic. Wherever possible, assets should be revalued at replacement cost and the trend in return on investment related to realistic valuations.

It is sometimes claimed that a revaluation of assets at annual intervals is far too costly. Yet an efficient business will revalue every year for the purposes of fire insurance. Annual fire insurance valuations would facilitate a quick revaluation of assets on a replacement basis and, where new fire insurance valuations are adopted each year, this series can be used as a means of reconstructing asset values.

The individual company may be able to examine asset records in this way, but few companies show replacement values for their assets in the balance sheet, so that the security analyst will be unable to base his assessment on up-to-date valuations. For this reason it is necessary to examine a range of other operating ratios in order to construct comparisons between companies and to obtain assessments of trends.

Pattern of analysis

It will be recognized that profits are generated from sales. Therefore the full analysis of a company's performance must embrace the whole of the company's operating experience from sales to costs in relation to assets. The pattern of analysis illustrating all the key relations leading up to return on capital employed was shown in Diagram 10.2. The advantage of adopting this kind of analysis is that, once a company's performance is shown in this way, the effect of changes in any particular factor or sets of factors can be worked through to illustrate changes in other relationships. For example, increases in costs can change disproportionately with increases in sales, depending upon the degree of capacity utilization. Therefore an increase in capacity which will require an increase in capital may result in a disproportionate increase in costs and a lower return on capital.

The analysis of ratios and trends can be made in great detail. A standard form of analysis is set out in Table 11.1. A working table of this kind must be completed for at least one business cycle. Since, as we have argued before, nearly every business reflects the developments of the cycle, and the cycle has been of roughly five years' duration, it is necessary to analyse the company's balance sheet and profit and loss account for the last five years, and preferably longer. In some cases, where the company is of large proportions, it will be advisable to go back for two cycles and to prepare a ten-year analysis. This is because major trends only change gradually and it is of considerable value to examine trends between one cycle and the next.

With regard to the reliability of asset values published in the company's annual accounts, it is sometimes argued that directors know best. The board will be better placed than outside observers with regard to the company's requirements in terms of replacement financing. If directors have made a correct assessment of depreciation requirements, it can be assumed that the gross profit after depreciation will be a realistic figure. Similarly, since the directors will have a good impression of the financing requirements of the company the extent of the dividend cover provided by earnings can be taken as a measure of the confidence directors have in the course of the company. Taken to its logical conclusion, then, the argument that directors know best leads to the position where the analyst need only concern himself with the dividend record and progression. This is precisely the view that had to be taken in the days before consolidated accounts were available. Experience has taught, however, that this view is, to say the least, naive and the analyst is obliged to examine depreciation provisions in relation to assets with considerable care.

It will be obvious from the methods outlined above that a thoroughgoing analysis is a lengthy procedure. Considerable time will be required to set out the details of the balance sheet and profit and loss account in a consistent way for a period as long as ten years. Even when this task is completed, analysis of ratios will absorb a great deal of time. In many cases it will be desirable to have a quick appraisal of the key trends in a company. In fact, it will be advisable to undertake a quick appraisal before embarking on a full-scale analysis, for in some instances the preliminary examination will show further examination to be pointless.

The key ratio for a quick appraisal is the marginal return on investment. It is possible to calculate the additional profit earned over a business cycle and to relate this to the increase in capital employed over the same period. To be

Table 11.1 A standard form of analysis

Income and profits	*Capital*	*Ratios*
1. Sales	17. Fixed assets at cost	30. Gross profit margin = 2 ÷ 1
2. Gross trading profit	18. Fixed assets at replacement cost	31. Sales/capital = 1 ÷ 23 or 28
3. *Plus: other income*	19. Fixed assets after depreciation	32. Sales/stock = 1 ÷ 20
4. Less: depreciation	20. Plus: stocks	33. Current liabilities/current assets
5. Less: interest	21. *Plus: other current assets*	(excluding stocks) = 22 ÷ 21
6. *Less: other debits*	22. *Less: current liabilities*	34. Tax ratio = 8 ÷ 7
7. Equal pre-tax profits	23. Equals: net capital employed[1]	35. Tax ratio/ruling rate of
8. *Less: tax*	24. Less: loan capital	corporation tax
9. Equals: net profit, after tax	25. Less: preference capital	36. Economic return on capital =
10. Less: minorities	26. *Less: Minority interest*	(2 ÷ 3) ÷ 28
11. *Less: preference dividends*	27. *Equals: net assets for ordinary*	37. Net pretax return on capital =
12. Equals: earnings available for	28. Gross capital employed[1]	7 ÷ 23 or 28
ordinary	= 18 + 20 + 21 − 22	38. Net return to equity = 12 ÷ 27
13. *Less: ordinary dividends*	29. Ordinary share capital	39. Payout ratio = 13 ÷ 12
14. Equals retained earnings		40. Cash flow/gross capital =
15. Plus depreciation		16 ÷ 28
16. Equals retained cash flow		41. Earnings per share = 12 ÷ 29
		42. Dividends per share (gross) =
		13 ÷ 29
		43. Cash flow, plus dividends per
		share = (16 + 13) ÷ 29

167

---

[1] Net capital employed as shown under item 23 corresponds to balance sheet presentation. Gross capital employed as shown under 28 includes fixed assets as estimated at replacement cost. For purposes of analysis, assets at replacement cost is a more meaningful parameter.

more exact, some allowance must be made for the time lag before assets become fully earning. Therefore the analysis of capital and profits should be lagged by – say – one year.

The analysis will appear as follows:

- Total capital employed in year 5 *minus* total capital employed in year 0 *equals* marginal increase in capital over the last business cycle.
- Gross profit, after depreciation and before tax and interest, in year 6 *minus* gross profit and so on in year 1 *equals* marginal increase in profits.
- Marginal return on marginal investment will be the increment of gross profit over the five-year period divided by the increment of capital.

This ratio indicating the marginal return on investment is an excellent indicator, particularly when compared with the average rate of return on total assets over the five-year period.

The message from this quick appraisal can be derived from a comparison of the marginal returns with the average returns. Where the marginal return diverges from the average, it may be assumed that the trends within the company are changing. If the marginal return is falling below the average return, this must be read as a warning signal for the future. Where the marginal return is greater than the average return, a better performance can be anticipated. However, the quick appraisal should only be used to identify positions which will then merit further study. In a situation which shows promise, the analyst must examine the underlying ratios to find the developments taking place in the company which confirm the conclusion that a better performance is under way. This quick method, therefore, is a means of sifting and identifying situations for the investment analyst to concentrate upon.

The importance of the historical record

Where the quick analysis shows that it will be worthwhile carrying out a full analysis and forecast of the company's profits, it is essential to read the annual reports and any other material, such as industry studies or investigations connected with monopoly enquiries, the company's sales brochures, catalogues and advertising material as well as prospectuses for capital issues. Where possible the search should go back ten years.

Details should be abstracted from the chairman's annual statements, not only for guidance on the changes in profitability, but for clues as to changes in policy and strategy. Details will be given as to diversification and expansion and also regarding problems where the company has suffered setbacks. As we have noted, a company diary is an extremely important tool, though if one existed no outsider is likely to be given access.

I recall a fellow analyst completing a major forecast of a company having gone back over ten years, getting into deep water when the irate chairman of the company in question, having read the draft, lodged a vitriolic complaint with our senior partner. In the event the analyst was completely vindicated when it was pointed out that the items to which the chairman had taken exception were all taken from the company's own annual reports. Memories can be rather short.

The forecaster should take account of what may be called 'boardroom psychology'. Where there is a change of chairmanship there is a fair chance that there will be a change in policy and in direction – for better or worse. Every chairman is motivated to make his mark on the company, leaving it in a stronger position at the end of his term of office than when he took over. Thus a chairman who is in a strong position and able to time his retirement or handing over, will strive to achieve a year of good results at the end of his term of office.

This may be easier said than done, since there must be something like a one in three chance that the fluctuations in the business cycle will deliver a bad year. Nevertheless, whether or not the outgoing chairman finishes on a bull or a bear note, the incoming chairman will endeavour to get adverse features into the open immediately. Write-offs and exceptional charges will, it is hoped, be laid at the door of the predecessor's term of office. The newcomer's first year may therefore show a turn for the worse, establishing a starting point where there is a better chance that profits will improve impressively through his term of office.

In interpreting the run of figures through the decade, the forecaster must make allowance for the quirks in boardroom changes. Where the chairmanship may have changed some years back, it will be clear from the chairman's annual statements whether or not the trend was bent. Where there has been a recent change in chairmanship, the interpretation of the company's position becomes more difficult. Nevertheless, it is prudent to assume that the newcomer will do his best to show himself in a good light at the end of his term.

Finalizing the forecast

Once the forecaster has familiarized himself with the company's history he is in a position to complete the lengthy process of setting out the year-by-year record of income, costs, profits, capital and operating ratios. Fund managers with a large staff of analysts will be able to justify the building of a computer program to digest the ten-year record and to spew out the relevant ratios and trends. A company analysing and forecasting its own performance may not be able to justify the cost of computerization unless it plans to build forecasts of other companies. In any event, suitable computer programs may be available for hire or purchase.

The first step, once the historical data and trends are available, is to relate that information to the trends in the economy as a whole. How do sales compare with the matching figures for the relevant sectors of consumer or capital spending across the board? That relationship is then projected through the forecasting period to the forecast of consumer or capital spending for the economy as a whole.

This process must be repeated for the salient items of costs and for gross profits. Where there is insufficient information on the company's costs, these can be estimated by subtracting the published gross profit figures from the sales revenue figures. The projections of the ratios of the cost and profit series against the projections for these items through the forecast will throw up forecasts for sales, costs and profits, which should be consistent. The chances are that the compound rates of change for the three items will not produce an exact match. The forecaster must then make minor adjustments to the projections to achieve consistency.

The single projections of the ratios must now be critically examined to check whether there are likely to be special factors in the company's performance which will alter the projected rates of change. Has the company made significant changes recently which are not yet reflected in the results? The company may have set in train a major investment programme, or have made a large acquisition, and if those investments were not paralleled in the company's ten-year history an allowance must be made for a step change in profits in the forecast period.

The forecasting technique is illustrated in the following hypothetical example (Table 11.2). The projections and forecasts must be continued for the other items in the cascade from interest, costs, depreciation, taxation, preference dividends, minorities, dividends for ordinary, retentions and cash flow.

This laborious but fascinating exercise produces an excellent test bed for checking the assumptions used in the forecast. The forecaster must take account of a natural bias towards optimism within the company, the board believing that its decisions are going to deliver the 'right' results.

The forecaster must also ensure that his enthusiasm does not equally carry him away, for it is not uncommon for the analyst to develop a parental interest in his work and to adopt a more favourable bias in the profit projections. It is an easy sleight of hand to make small adjustments in one or two ratios to generate a more optimistic outcome.

Conclusions

- The connection between share prices and the profit cycle underscores the need to have reliable forecasts of the company sector as a whole.

Table 11.2 Sales forecast (per cent per annum)

		By value	Price	By volume[1]
A	The company's sales growth, 1990/2000	5·3	1·7	3·5
B	Consumers' spending, 1990/2000	4·5	2·0	2·5
C	Ratio of A to B	1·18	0·85	1·40
D	Consumers' spending 2000/2005	4·50	1·80	2·70
E	Forecast ratios	1·20	0·83	1·42
F	Company's sales D × E	5·40	1·50	3·84

1 The volume figures are derived by dividing the growth rate in value by the growth rate in prices; i.e. $1·053 \div 1·017 = 1·035$.

- The national income accounts factor incomes data are a more reliable basis for estimating company sector gross profits than series built up from samples of company accounts.
- The company profits series shows a clear cyclical pattern and provides some guidance in determining turning points in share prices.
- A profit forecast can be checked by subtracting the forecast of costs from the forecast of sales.
- It can also be forecast by tracing the relationship between movements in the economy as a whole and the sharper cyclical movements in profits.
- In an analysis of the economy and the company sector as a whole, labour costs are the most important factor. Particular attention should be paid to the development of wage rates.
- Where available, the input/output tables by industrial sector in the national accounts give information as to the relative size (weights) of the various cost factors.
- The forecast of gross trading profits can be expanded by adding rent and non-trading income as well as income from abroad. Then the deductions for depreciation, interest and taxation determine the balance attributable to shareholders in the form of earnings per share.
- This cascade analysis also yields a figure for cash flow which has a great influence on investment decisions both within the firm and in security analysis.
- In profit forecasting for a company it is essential to calculate the gross return obtained on the total stock of assets. This provides a measure of efficiency in the management of assets.
- The return to shareholders is calculated by relating earnings after tax to shareholders' net assets.

- Particular care should be taken in checking balance sheet asset values. Ideally, these should be based on the annual estimates derived from fire insurance replacement values.
- When it comes to the publication of company accounts, it is not advisable to assume that 'directors know best'.
- In analysing other companies, a quick calculation of the marginal return on capital employed can save time and filter out those companies not worth a full and lengthy analysis.
- It is essential to read annual reports and all other relevant material going back as far as ten years to identify changes in policy and strategy.
- The forecaster must make allowances for 'boardroom psychology' and the effects of changes in chairmanship.

Sources

Security Analysis (Graham *et al.*).

Investment Analysis (Weaver).

Forecasting Company Profits (Wellings).

National income accounts.

12 FORECASTING SHARE PRICES

The attempt to forecast share prices is the most demanding and exciting of all forecasting exercises. The task falls into three parts. First, it is necessary to forecast movements in the market as a whole. Then an attempt must be made to identify and predict the cyclical excesses of the market. Finally, forecasts of particular share prices have to be constructed in the context of the overall market movements.

The movements in the international and domestic markets are, of course, beyond the control of the firm. A company, however, can influence its own share price. In a sense the management is always striving to do that so as to raise the share price, and it is hoped, to outperform the market.

The big picture

The development of credit banking in Holland during the 17th century, followed by Britain, helped finance the growth of commerce and international trade. Share markets only became significant in the 19th century. The progress towards an efficient capital market was interrupted by the collapse of the Mississippi and South Sea bubbles early in the 18th century. Those setbacks delayed the development of a capitalist system based on the joint stock company with limited liability.

In the 19th century, the great majority of companies remained in private hands. The number of companies quoted on the American and European markets was tiny compared with the position at the end of the 20th century. The expansion of markets gathered pace with the increase in taxation. The weight of death duties forced family-owned companies to go public and the severe load of taxation in the First World War reinforced that trend.

We now have a vast international capital market, heavily dominated by the USA. It follows, therefore, that attention is focused on movements in US share prices and the prospects for that market. The most critical factor is the weight of money available for investment. It is literally true in a capitalist system that money makes the world go round. A shortage of cash leads to a weak share market and vice versa.

The logic of this stems from the role of interest rates. Short-term rates are directly under the control of the central bank or the government. Bank rate may be raised in an attempt to curb, or reduce, the demand for credit. A high level of interest rates will reduce the demand for credit and the growth in the money supply. In those conditions businesses and consumers are faced with a rise in interest payments and are forced to economize. Investment projects are pruned back, the housing market weakens and sales of durables fall.

The change in the business climate is a clear indication that profits will weaken. Firms will be forced to cut back, laying off labour and raising unemployment. Household spending will also be curbed and this combination of cyclical events will be reflected in a downturn of the share market.

In fact, the market generally leads, since rising interest rates constitute a clear warning and investors will reduce their commitments, taking profits in some cases and preferring to hold cash. The market can also suffer from forced sales by companies of minority stakes held in other companies. In a severe credit squeeze these sales have a significant downward effect on share prices.

It is therefore extremely important to keep an eye on the monthly money supply figures. Where the growth in the money supply is faster than the growth in national income, measured in market prices, the excess indicates that, if it is sustained, business conditions will improve, spending growth will accelerate, profits growth will also expand and share prices will rise. The investor should therefore maintain a constant watch on changes in interest rates and money supply and the expectations of future changes in money supply.

It requires no more than a quick daily digest of the financial news to keep abreast of events and to be prepared for the occasional changes in direction of the share markets. Over the long run the phases of rising share prices (bull markets) outrun the bear markets by a wide margin.

Long phases and bubbles

Apart from the cyclical movements in the economy and the share markets, economic management runs in long phases, as was illustrated in Diagram 2.1. Economic doctrine evolves over lengthy periods, one fashion gradually replacing another. What begins as a piece of academic economic theory filters through in the course of discussion and debate into acceptance at the political level.

Thus the political economy is managed *à la mode* so that from the 1920s the capitalist world has seen swings in fiscal, monetary and exchange rate management at intervals as long as 30 years. These changes are relevant to the capital markets and the great concern at the effects of the Wall Street crash of the early 1930s and the worldwide economic slump led to measures to regulate markets, banking, money and exchange rates. As a result, the prolonged post-1945 recovery and expansion was accompanied by a prolonged bull market punctuated by no more than modest downturns.

As economic management swung towards laissez-faire monetarism in the 1970s, markets became more volatile. Then, in the 1990s, the liberalization of the capital markets following the dismantling of exchange controls led to greater emphasis on fiscal discipline and the elimination of price inflation. Against that background there has been a progressive globalization of capital markets and the evolution of a world economy which has lessened the economic sovereignty of national governments.

This phase is likely to be long-lasting. Yet market globalization, in a world where the Internet ensures that investors imbibe the same diet of financial, economic and political news day by day, promises to intensify their herd-like behaviour. The chances are, therefore, that share markets, led by the USA, will become more volatile and, to that extent, more dangerous.

The conditions have thus become more propitious for the development of stock market bubbles, those hitherto infrequent episodes where speculation intensifies, greed increases and bystanders are drawn into a gambling frenzy. In those bubbles prices are driven to unjustifiable and unsustainable levels at which the wise take profits and the foolish Johnny-come-latelies lose their shirts.

Why bubbles develop at particular times is difficult to say. Tulip mania in Holland in the 1630s, sparked by the import of an exotic Turkish flower, coincided with the growing wealth of the Dutch merchant community. Money and credit were available to fund speculation and the bursting of the bubble did not interrupt the growth of Dutch trade and commerce.

Nearly a hundred years later, however, the related Mississippi and South Sea bubbles in France and Britain collapsed after such frenetic levels of speculation that the political backlash put a substantial brake on the development of the capitalist system.

In France, the huge extravagance of Louis XIV virtually bankrupted the state. On his death the national debt was vast in relation to the tax revenues. In the crisis, John Law, an inveterate Scottish gambler, propounded a scheme aimed at expanding credit and trade by linking the issuance of paper notes to specie, with the note issue linked to a land bank. Law gained the ear of the Regent and in the event was authorized in 1716 to establish a bank whose notes would be accepted in payment of taxes. All the notes were made payable at sight and in the coin current at the time they were issued.

This shrewd move raised the value of the notes above the value of precious metals and firmly established the reputation of Law's bank, laying the foundation for what became a vast bubble of credit and paper inflation. In 1719 the Mississippi Company was formed with exclusive rights of trading in Louisiana with its alleged abundance of precious metals. The speculative frenzy led to the issue of shares and notes on a massive scale, the government, in its greed to eradicate the national debt, failing to meet Law's original prudence in maintaining an asset backing for the note issue.

In London, the South Sea Company was formed in 1711 with the aim of restoring public credit. A company of merchants took on some £10 million of national debt, the government paying a rate of interest of 6 per cent. To raise the wind the government made certain duties permanent and granted the monopoly of trade to the South Seas to the company.

Thus the background and origins of the two bubbles were similar. The South Sea Company had ambitions to trade with Spanish America and to be repaid in gold and silver. The first ship set sail in 1717, but in the following year the trade was suppressed. The South Sea Company and the Bank of England then proposed to parliament to increase the capital stock. Demand for stock was strong and the initial success of the Mississippi flotation in Paris encouraged speculation in London. In 1720, a proposal to redeem the whole of the national debt was received with great enthusiasm and the bubble in South Sea stock expanded rapidly.

More and more stock was issued at rising prices and in the wake of speculation in South Sea shares a wide range of other new ventures was launched. Gold was transferred to London from all parts of the country and when the crash came the South Sea Company brought other businesses down with it. The mushrooming of new issues was not dissimilar to the Internet and new technology fever of the 1999 bubble.

Neither the Mississippi nor the South Sea bubbles hold lessons for today's investor except to provide a warning against being caught up in a speculative frenzy. Yet it is as well to remember that every transaction involves a buyer and a seller and that, as share prices escalate upwards in a bubble period, sellers make substantial profits. One such was Thomas Guy, whose profits on South Sea stock led to the foundation of the hospital, now world-famous, bearing his name.

In retrospect, therefore, a bubble generates an unusual volume of profits and losses and to a large extent the underlying economy is not necessarily damaged. However, the drama of the bubble's collapse and the extent of the fall in price of bubble stock shares stays in the public memory. The previous profits tend to be overlooked. The investor should not venture into a bubble speculation unless the discipline of taking a profit on the way up can be rigorously upheld.

There was a further landmark bubble in the 19th century centred on the formation and expansion of British railway companies. Expectations were again pitched far too high. The overbuilding resulted in intense competition and poor profitability which persisted well into the 20th century. In that respect railway development mirrored the wave of canal building late in the 18th century. The cost inflation of the Napoleonic wars ruined the chances of a profitable outcome of the later canal developments. Ultimately, canal companies were bought by rail companies who then used the canal routes, gradually squeezing the canals out of business.

The bubble in the 1890s, arising from the discovery of the South African goldfields, had a wider economic impact in that, under the operation of the gold standard, the production of gold raised the world's money supply, helping expand spending and output. The bubbles in the uranium stocks in the 1950s and nickel in the 1970s had little economic impact.

The force of the credit multiplier

Thus the forecaster has to distinguish between the characteristics of bubbles. Those which inflict deep damage are rare. Unquestionably, the US bubble in the fashionable car and radio stocks of the 1920s and the mounting speculation financed on margins, which embraced the whole market, had a catastrophic outcome. The major lesson lay in the gullibility of bankers in fuelling the credit explosion. The credit multiplier is extremely powerful and the banking law that 'every advance creates its own deposit' should never be forgotten. When a borrower draws cheques against a loan those cheques are paid into the banking system, raising deposits and enabling the recipient banks to increase their lending. At the end of the day the initial loan is matched by the rise in deposits and money supply.

The moral of that tragedy is that nation states need well-informed and powerful central banks mandated to maintain the value of money. This entails curbing the growth in credit and money supply. Sadly, the credit expansion of the 1920s was unregulated. Perversely, the government failed to stem the collapse which followed by expanding the money supply and spending power.

The lessons have been learned, however, and the structure and institutions of the world recovery since 1945 have evolved to the point where damaging credit explosions can be avoided. But this does not guarantee that central banks – and the governments which they answer to – read the signs correctly and act quickly enough and forcefully enough to prevent inflationary credit cycles and bubbles developing.

We repeat, therefore, that the forecaster must pay great attention to the monetary statistics for signs of erratic movements which may have consequences for share markets as a whole, as well as for particular sectors.

Evaluating the market

Although the forecaster is likely to be concerned with the prospects for individual companies, there are occasions when the likelihood of a fall in the market as a whole must be taken into account. There are a few occasions when a bear market is so pervasive that virtually no stock stands up against the wind. Thus, when forecasting for a particular company, the analyst will be expected to have formed a view of the likely movement of the market as a whole and the conditions likely to prevail should a takeover bid be contemplated.

It is essential, therefore, to establish a set of yardsticks for the evaluation of market levels. This inevitably entails historical analysis and a logical appraisal of the rationale of investment. In buying a stock the investor acquires the title to a stream of future income. That potential flow must be assessed against the level of interest rates. Interest rates measure the price of money. Thus the higher the rate of interest the higher the potential income growth from shares to justify a purchase. Put the other way round, rising interest rates will tend to depress share prices.

Shares have a higher risk factor than government bonds. In addition, the dealing costs in buying and selling shares are higher. Share prices, therefore, have to reflect this risk factor. This means that the yield from shares, after allowing for the potential growth in dividends and the share price, has to exceed the income yield from government bonds by two percentage points or more.

Where the company concerned is in a highly volatile industry, heavily dependent on credit, such as housing or consumer durables, the risk factor will be greater. In broad terms the arithmetic of the equation is as follows:

Assume	starting dividend yields of	3 per cent
	long-term growth rate	5 per cent
	long-term yield	8 per cent
	equity risk factor	2 per cent
	long-term bond yield	6 per cent

In this example, where the bond yield is 6 per cent, a lower starting dividend yield and/or a lower growth rate will not yield sufficient to cover the assumed risk factor. This shows that, on the assumptions underlying the forecast, the share price is too high.

The importance of earnings per share

The company's ability to generate income for its shareholders is encapsulated in its earnings per share. Conventionally, analysts have relied on dividend growth as the key measure of the company's potential and its future share price. Yet there are two reasons for taking a broader view.

In recent years there has been a growing tendency for companies to use share buy-back as a means of channelling cash to their shareholders in preference to paying dividends. This is in part due to the taxation of dividend income in some countries being heavier than capital gains taxes. It is notable, for example, that the American colossus, Microsoft, has never paid a dividend. Neither has Warren Buffet's extraordinary investment company Berkshire Hathaway.

Dividend yields across the world have fallen well below the long-term averages of the modern capitalist era from the First World War. This does not necessarily mean that all shares are overvalued. More to the point, it is essential to concentrate on the earnings per share measure as the basis of analysis and judgement.

In this respect historical comparisons of earnings and share price/earnings ratios (P/Es) need careful interpretation. Since a business has to replace its assets it has to set aside funds every year in the form of depreciation provisions to replace those assets when the time comes. Whether or not those provisions are sufficient to meet the replacement costs will depend on the changes in price of the assets in question as well as the change in technology.

If, for example, the average life of the company's assets (machinery, plant, buildings and transport) is 13 years, it is possible to construct a profile of replacement cost and to compare that with the accumulated depreciation provision over that period. Since we are considering an on-going business, the depreciation cash flow will be invested in the business year by year. On a long-term average the expectation would be that those funds would generate a return for the firm of 7–8 per cent net of tax.

For the average company this would be sufficient to offset a rise in asset prices of around 3–4 per cent per annum. Thus, in any 13-year period where the inflation rate exceeds this level, the inflation provisions would be inadequate and the company would need to draw from its after-tax earnings for the equity shareholders. This logically suggests that in periods of high inflation P/E ratios will tend to be lower since part of the earnings has to supplement the depreciation provision. Conversely, periods of low inflation, averaging less than 3 per cent per annum, will result in a surplus in accumulated depreciation provision. This margin will supplement earnings and P/E ratios will be above the long-term average.

The market ratios bear out this feature, P/E ratios being lower in the wake of wartime inflation, higher in the 1960s, lower again in response to the high inflation of the 1970s and 1980s and higher again later in the 1990s and into the 2000s.

The phase of low inflation beginning in the 1990s will be reinforced by the worldwide expansion of business-to-business Internet transactions. Asset replacement costs are likely to be held down and in the electronics field many replacements will be at lower prices. For this reason P/E ratios are more likely to be significantly higher than the long-run averages, and with justification.

In evaluating the overall market levels, the cyclical movements and the occasional bubbles, these factors affecting earnings and dividends should be kept in mind. In forecasting a company's performance and share price, its earnings per share and dividend per share growth rates have to be compared with those of the market as a whole, both historically and through the forecast period.

An irrational market

The company has to assess profits and earnings per share for internal analysis and planning and in connection with acquisitions. The analyst has to forecast profits and earnings for portfolio investment purposes. Both the individual company and the security analyst have the common problem of evaluating share prices. Where takeovers and mergers are concerned, interest will be concentrated upon share prices in the short run. In fact, much of the attention paid to the market will continue to be concentrated on short-run movements. Nevertheless, it is also necessary to have a long-term assessment of trends and the appropriate share price in order to relate current developments to some normal set of yardsticks.

It cannot be denied that, over a long run of years, share prices as a whole reflect developments in profits as a whole. Whilst the forecaster has to adopt a rational, logical approach to arrive at a profile of the likely share prices, it has to be acknowledged that markets are not perfect, even though the flow of information on companies has improved and is available to all those with time to read.

It is of considerable importance to relate the experience of a company to that of the whole economy in order to assess relative profit performance. The relative profit and earnings performance will be reflected through the market in the relative share price behaviour. Thus it is possible to measure how the market has capitalized a company's profits, earnings and dividends in the past. This can be done for the various stages in the business cycle and, since all companies experience cyclical movements of one kind or another, an analysis of share price movements and yield movements is required for at least one full cycle.

The reason why it is essential in share price evaluation to measure the performance of the company against the market as a whole lies in the belief that the market itself is the repository of most relevant knowledge at any point of time. The evidence points to the apparent ability of the market to glean information about a company's progress and to reflect this progress in the share price well in advance of any publication of such data. An individual share price, therefore, is likely to reflect much more relevant knowledge than any single analyst can sometimes bring to bear on the company in question. In most cases the market itself, though far from infallible, is likely to be more right than wrong.

This view would appear to be invalid when the sharp movements in share prices from year to year are examined. A share price is no more than the price at which a buyer and seller are brought together. In fact, an individual share price on any particular day has very little to do with the fundamental values which are generally attributed to share prices. There are various reasons which lead to the sale of a share and the personal motives are frequently important. Shares are sold, perhaps regardless of timing, to meet death duty obligations. The pressure on liquidity will also lead to the sale of shares, and sometimes at disadvantageous points in the business cycle. Disillusion can lead to the sale of a share at precisely the point at which it would be profitable to buy.

In addition, the factors contributing to the purchase of shares must not be overlooked. Since institutional investors are very important in this sphere of activity, it is to be hoped that more rational reasons prevail. However, it is worth noting that peak sales of unit trusts to the public, for example, have occurred at the top of the business cycle rather than at the bottom. From the movements of share prices in general it is obvious that the overall liquidity position in the economy is of the greatest importance in determining the overall level of share prices.

Because of these differing motives for transactions, many companies experience swings in their share price during the course of the year which throw up wide disparities between the high and low points. On this evidence it must be concluded that at some times during the course of a year a share price is well out of line with its appropriate level. An additional explanation for extreme movements can be found in the natural tendency in any market for opinion to swing in an exaggerated fashion from one point to another.

The level of share prices is, therefore, only a guide to fundamental values over long periods of time. Since factors such as political sentiment, tax changes and international developments can affect the level of the market for a period of years, it is not even feasible to take one business cycle with another in determining fundamental values.

Against this background, is it really possible to say that share prices are rational? When the relatively short history of the joint stock company is examined together with the major uncertainties surrounding share markets over the past hundred years, it may well be questioned whether there are any lessons to be learned.

Identifying anomalies

Individual share prices often diverge from the market averages, or norms, for a variety of reasons. A basic benchmark for share markets is provided by the long-term average growth rates of earnings and dividends per share and the dividend yield. Assuming a state of equilibrium, the capital yield from an equity investment is reflected in the growth rate in earnings per share. Thus, taking a period of one year and a growth rate of 5 per cent, that growth will be mirrored in the growth in the share price. After one year the capital value will have risen from 100 to 105. If the shares are sold at the end of the year, the total yield will have been 5 per cent plus the dividends received during the year. Typically, this would result in a total yield of around 7 per cent before allowing for taxation.

In a perfect economic and market system this market yield should match the performance of the companies generating the underlying profits. This pattern of yields is as follows:

Equity capital employed	100
Gross return after depreciation	15
less: corporation tax	7
available for ordinary	8
less: dividends	3
retained = growth rate	5
Capital at year end	105

From this assessment share prices would, in the long-run, move up by an average of 5 per cent per annum. Financial engineering (discussed below) may, however, improve the return and a combination of leverage (gearing), share buy-backs and the use of share options will raise the average growth potential to – say – 6 per cent.

By identifying the underlying trends in operation for the market as a whole and comparing these with an individual company's performance, it is possible to identify share price anomalies. Once the previous relationships between a company and its share price and the market as a whole have been identified, forecasts of both can be made in preparation for a forecast of future share prices. In most cases it will be impossible to assert whether a share price is too high or too low unless a forecast of the overall market level has been prepared as a basis for detailed evaluation. Empirical observation indicates that the majority of share prices are only out of line in the short run and that the market begins to pull the share price back into line within a relatively short period.

In order to optimize investment timing, a great deal of attention should be paid to the question of short-term divergencies away from normal price. Therefore, once the forecast for the market as a whole has been established and the relationships between the company profit record, earnings and dividends per share and the market as a whole have been established for the past, the estimates of the company's future performance can be used as a means of constructing a share price forecast. When this has been completed the analyst must assess the reliability of the forecast. In all cases some idea of the uncertainties and risks entailed can be established by measuring the range within which the forecasts are likely to lie. It will also be necessary to assess the varying degrees of probability which can be attached to forecasts for different companies and shares.

Since there is such a vast range of securities available for selection, it is virtually impossible to sift and check such huge numbers of ratios and comparisons by hand. The computer is an ideal tool for storing data about the past so that the process of search can be speeded up dramatically. It is possible to survey the whole range of alternatives and to make many forms of comparisons with the aid of the computer. All the ratios listed in the previous chapter can be recorded on the computer and, provided the analyst can state his investment criteria, a computer can be used to select stocks which fit this norm. However, the computer can only select from the data which it has been given with regard to the past. In practice a share price is, to some extent, a measure of future expectations. A share is a title to the future stream of income and the price paid for a share is an evaluation of a kind of forecast of the expected future stream of income.

Future expectations are not the only element to determine a share price. Apart from the irrational, personal motives, a number of factors can be identified which influence the market. To start with the obvious, past performance and future expectations of both dividends and earnings must have considerable weight. Since dividends are not the sole evidence of capacity to pay, dividend cover is another variable to be considered. The volatility of earnings and dividends is of particular importance. The motor industry, for example, has an above-average volatility, profits swinging from around zero at the bottom of the cycle to fat levels at the top. The uncertainty as to both earnings and, to a lesser extent, dividends is plainly reflected in the disparity of both the starting and the long-term yields of the industry.

Similarly, takeover possibilities may be reflected in a share price and a share price may be too high or not justified by current earnings because the market recognizes greater potential in the underlying assets or because a bid has been made, or hinted at, in the past. In more cases than not, a rumour of a bid is in time substantiated.

Finally, there is the question of politics. The risks fall under two heads, home and foreign. At home the chances of government intervention with such things as subsidies and tax changes are reflected in prices. Abroad the degree of stability is a key factor.

These will be the major items which can be identified in a broad analysis of share prices. Even so, they will not explain price levels completely, for there will be individual characteristics such as the age and composition of the management, dominant personal shareholdings, where a death could lead to a massive disposal of shares, overdependence on one man in management, and so on, all of which could be reflected in the share price.

The main factors likely to influence a share price may therefore be summarized as follows:

- the earnings record
- the dividend record
- the dividend cover
- the volatility of earnings
- the dividend yield
- the earnings yield
- management factors
- political factors
- asset value per share
- expected growth in earnings
- expected growth in dividends.

It is probable that the most important of these items are future growth expectations and volatility. The profit forecasts must therefore be of considerable value, and are indispensable in the overall assessment of the potential share price.

Share price charts

The fluctuations in a company's share price are well illustrated in a chart of its daily movements. Financial services companies maintain charts and these are available via computer printouts. There are also specialist firms which produce and analyse share price charts, interpreting the movements to make predictions of future prices.

In evaluating and forecasting a share price it is advisable to check the underlying earnings per share history against the share price chart. The price movements will in most cases be greater than the fluctuations in earnings and this evidence must be taken into account in finalizing the share price forecast.

Financial engineering

Company managers have increasingly focused attention on share prices in recent years and this has led to attempts to boost earnings per share by various moves bracketed under the label of financial engineering.

Leverage, in the form of borrowing from the bank or the issue of bonds, has always been a feature of company financing. It is a general practice to use bank loans or overdrafts to finance inventories and working capital. From the bank's point of view the risks are modest, since stocks and work-in-progress result in sales revenue in a matter of months.

The leverage engineered via the issue of fixed interest bonds is an attractive means of increasing earnings per share since it is usually the case that the company's return on capital employed is significantly greater than the rate of interest payable on the bonds. That margin contributes directly to enhancing the return on shareholders' funds.

Yet leverage is not without its risks, notably in those cases where sales are volatile. The credit-dependent industries, such as house and property development, cars and household durables, are subject to large swings in profitability as a direct consequence of the cycle in interest rates. When rates are high, depressing spending, profits will tumble. This results in the return on capital employed falling below the rate of interest payable on the company's bond issues. Earnings per share are therefore reduced as a result of the bond leverage.

The riskiness of leverage is substantial in these cases and this is reflected in the share price. Thus, although the average return on capital employed may be up to the general average, or even higher, the volatility of the earnings leads to a lower rating and valuation of the company's shares.

By contrast, in businesses in industries where the cyclical volatility is small, such as food retailing, leverage can more safely be employed since the fluctuations in return on capital employed are unlikely to take the return on equity below the interest rate payable on the bonds. As a result the company's shares are valued on a higher basis than the more cyclical stocks, even though the leverage factor may be higher.

Share buy-backs, increasing in popularity, are virtually risk-free. The reduction of the number of shares in issue will, of itself, marginally increase the potential share price. On a longer view the return on the undiminished body of assets is spread over fewer shares. Hence earnings per share is increased. Simultaneously, leverage is increased in those cases where the company has issued bonds.

Finally, the use of share options as rewards, to motivate a company's top executives to deliver in terms of enhancing the share price, is now fairly general. Options are issued on terms that are related to share price performance. The options may be worthless if the share price fails to reach a specified level by a specified date. The executive may be very handsomely rewarded if the price exceeds the targets by a good margin.

The motivation may generate gains to the executives which shareholders believe to be too generous. In the majority of cases, shareholders are content to see attention focused on cost saving, which generally means reducing numbers employed, and a combination of policies rationalizing products, production and sales. It will also involve financial engineering in the shape of leverage and share buy-backs.

All these features of financial engineering must be kept in mind in forecasting share prices. For the individual company, a share price forecast will be essential to the design of a share option package. The option price will need to be set in relation to the initial share price forecast. Where a company is contemplating a merger or an acquisition it will also need share price forecasts for both the immediate future and the longer term – say five years.

In analysing and forecasting share prices of other companies it is also necessary to question whether financial engineering is a major feature or whether it is likely to be stepped up in future. Forecasts for use in portfolio management, or in the search for potential acquisitions, must follow the same principles and it is essential to compile an analysis of a company's history, its volatility, its relationship to the economy and share market at large and market status as revealed by the chart of its share price movements.

The complexity of the exercise calls for the utmost in terms of judgement and skills. It is the most challenging of forecasting exercises and by far the most stimulating and exciting.

Conclusions

- The strength of a share market depends upon cash. The stock market generally leads the business cycle. The investor should maintain a constant watch on changes in interest rates and money supply.
- The share markets, led by the USA, are likely to become more volatile with the continuing globalization of the economies and the dissemination of financial news. Stock market bubbles are likely to become more frequent.
- When forecasting a particular company, the analyst must form a view of the likely movement of the share market as a whole.
- Earnings per share is the key measure of a company's performance and a crucial factor in forecasting its share price.
- In periods of high inflation, P/Es will tend to be lower, and vice versa.

- Low inflation and replacement of electronic products at lower prices will justify P/E ratios higher than the historic averages.
- Over a long run of years, share prices reflect developments in profits as a whole. Nevertheless, markets are not perfect and share price movements are often irrational.
- An analysis of share price and yield movements should be carried out for at least one full cycle in relation to the market as a whole.
- In many cases share prices swing substantially during the course of a year, throwing up wide disparities between the highs and the lows.
- By identifying the underlying trends for the market as a whole and comparing these with an individual company's performance, it is possible to identify short-term anomalies.
- The most important items determining a share price are future growth expectations and volatility.
- Share price charts are an indispensable aid in forming a judgement on a share price.
- Financial engineering via leverage, share buy-backs and options is an important factor bearing on future share prices.

Sources

Manias, Panics and Crashes: A History of Financial Crises (Kindleberger).

Common Stocks and Uncommon Profits (Fisher).

The Battle for Investment Survival (Loeb).

A Short History of Financial Euphoria (Galbraith).

The Great Crash 1929 (Galbraith).

Extraordinary Popular Delusions and the Madness of Crowds (Mackay).

Value Investing Made Easy: Benjamin Graham's Classic Investment Strategy

Explained for Everyone (Lowe).

Letters to Shareholders (Buffet).

The South Sea Bubble (Carswell).

The Art of Investment (Ellinger); an explanation of chart analysis.

The General Theory of Employment, Interest and Money (Keynes); see in particular Chapter 12.

The Economic Background to Investment (Rose).

13 THE RULES OF FORECASTING

A forecast of the business environment and of the specific features vital to a firm's success embraces a wide range of subjects. There are, however, a set of simple rules and guidelines that should be kept in mind in all forecasting, whether for business or for the diverse fields of weather, gambling or the sciences. The principle rules are given below.

The future has its roots in the past

The future grows out of the past. We therefore have to know the past and to interpret the unfolding trends and changes in order to make an intelligent projection into the future. Keep a diary of the major political and economic events as well as a diary of the company, recording the significant factors affecting its performance.

Forecasts are dependent upon their underlying assumptions

The uncertainties surrounding the future mean that the various strands from the past can strengthen or weaken in the future. The interaction between various forces can change. It is therefore essential to set down the assumptions on which the forecast is constructed. It may be necessary to use different sets of assumptions to test their impact on the forecasts. This will give an indication of the range of risk.

Forecasts are also dependent upon the historical data, which may be subject to wide margins of error

As any historian will tell you, there are various interpretations of history. Apart from the difficulties of establishing the facts, which are quite substantial regarding the recent past, let alone the long-time past, prejudices and different viewpoints will generate different interpretations.

In that respect the received versions of history are not necessarily foolproof starting points for evaluating trends. In the fields of economics and social surveys, sampling techniques are far from perfect and the end result may have a wide margin of uncertainty. This also applies in the medical field, though the danger of drawing wrong conclusions from an inadequate sample, or poor measurements, means that sampling is usually on a large scale and may be carried out over long periods.

Always, therefore, check the basis of a set of statistics to gauge its likely accuracy. In most cases the series will be inaccurate. This means that the prudent forecaster will use a variety of sources to obtain cross-checks and to narrow down the range of uncertainty.

Garbage in equals garbage out

If unreliable data are used in compiling the forecast, the forecast is likely to be worthless. The relationships derived will prove to be castles built upon sand. Dustbin relationships are to be avoided like the plague.

Major trends only change gradually

The fundamental aspects of life are very slow to change. Work, diet and lifestyles, for example, are deeply entrenched aspects of human activity and are seldom subject to sudden or drastic changes. Leisure activities and fashions are subject to faster rates of change. Human nature is virtually unchangeable.

Spending decisions depend upon cash

Forecasters occasionally overlook the importance of cash and spending power. This may happen where a single product is being considered. The forecaster must remember that the spending of each individual and society as a whole is constrained by the amount of cash available at any point of time. All products and services are in a sense in competition for the potential customer's spending power.

Cash equals confidence

Economic optimism (or pessimism) is determined by how well-off a person feels. When we are short of cash, or in financial difficulties, we are understandably depressed and lacking in confidence. Thus all surveys of confidence, whether of consumers or of business people, reflect their relative cash position. When the cash position is better than usual, confidence is higher than usual.

Confidence surveys, therefore, tell us about the availability of cash at the time the survey was taken. They are a leading indicator so far as forecasting is concerned where the results from month to month show a change in trend either upwards or downwards. Similar information can be gleaned from the monthly money supply figures and the two series should be compared for confirmation of a change in direction.

In the majority of cases it is true to say that 'money burns holes in people's pockets'. The discipline of voluntary saving is hard to maintain for many people and windfalls are more often spent than saved.

Financial change can be immediate; physical change is slow

One of the forecaster's biggest problems is to detect changes in trend and the timing of those changes. In the financial markets change can be as quick as a thought for the simple reason that we have to do no more than pick up a phone to place an order to buy or sell foreign currency, shares or bonds.

Financial markets can change direction rapidly, in a matter of hours or days, whereas in the physical world of making things change is slow. It may take a board of directors months to change an investment programme in the light of a changing business environment. Then there are further time lags as orders for plant and machinery are expanded or cut and for these changes to be made to levels of production. Many financial analysts and forecasters do not allow enough for the time lags at work in the real world as distinct from the financial world.

One business cycle generates the next
A business cycle is a period of several years characterized by a phase of above-average growth followed by a deceleration with a period of below-average growth or recession in which output falls.

These swings are brought about by changes in the world economy, dominated by the USA and by domestic changes in fiscal and monetary policy. In the democracies, where elections are either at fixed intervals or for limited terms, there is an above-average chance that the party in office will time changes in fiscal policy – cutting taxes and raising government spending – so as to influence an election.

The swings in one business cycle generate the next business cycle and it is extremely difficult for governments and central banks to coordinate policies in such a way as to flatten out and smooth away the business cycle.

Statistics describe people and human activity
When using statistical series, such as the national income accounts, it is easy to forget that the tables are an attempt to measure the sum of individual human activity. People's hopes, aspirations, fears, needs, wants and achievements are encapsulated in most statistical series. The aggregates are imperfect measures, not least because of the problem of sampling individuals and businesses.

Man is a dynamic animal: allow for his reaction to problems
The forecaster must take human motivation into account. In bad times, such as economic recession or natural disasters, news is presented in a dramatic way so that it is difficult to guess at the possibilities of recovery.

Man, as a species, is a highly successful surviving animal. We are programmed to survive and the majority of people have the capacity to face up to problems. If the problems are serious enough, we bestir ourselves and take action. On balance, therefore, the forecaster should be biased to a modest extent towards optimism rather than pessimism.

Today's best becomes tomorrow's norm
'Keeping up with the Joneses' describes the tendency for the spending patterns of the richer echelons to be copied by the lower echelons in society. It is an astonishing fact that the personal comfort enjoyed by the majority of people in western society is substantially greater than that enjoyed by monarchs in the 19th century. Personal transport in the shape of the car,

central heating, comfortable housing, household appliances, sanitation, health services and leisure facilities, all form the basis of a lifestyle of unbelievable comfort compared with generations of a century ago.

It is in that sense that 'today's best becomes tomorrow's norm'. The best in terms of quality and design now percolates down through society at a faster pace, helped by the instantaneous supply of information on new products and by the compound growth in spending power and access to credit.

The improvements in building design and construction and in industrial technology lead to the high-quality products in all walks of life being gradually adopted as the common standard or norm.

Never overlook the weather and natural forces

For all the increase in man's knowledge and technology, the forces of nature are vast and the lives of many millions of people in different parts of the world are constantly under threat from drought, famine, flood, and volcanic and earthquake activity, let alone the perils of pestilence and disease.

The growing salinity of the Australian continent is a current example of a destructive natural force, resulting in large measure from human activity. Although man's knowledge and understanding of the earth's climate will increase, there is little prospect of thwarting or preventing these excesses of rainfall and drought. These natural events have always had a major impact on man's economic activities and this will continue to be the case. Part of the cyclical rhythm of economic life derives from the climatic cycles.

Break down rather than build up

In compiling forecasts it is, in most cases, better to forecast the total and then to disaggregate that figure into the component parts. This applies most obviously to the breakdown of a market into the market share of its producers. Adding up each firm's prediction of its market share invariably sums to more than 100 per cent.

Equally, when forecasting an aggregate, such as the gross domestic product (GDP), it is advisable to forecast the total from past trends and anticipated changes in the world economy, fiscal and monetary policy and then to forecast the component parts of spending (demand), production and incomes. The estimates of the components have to be reconciled with the forecast total. Even where computerized models are used there are 'residual' items which have to be manipulated by judgement to reconcile the parts with the total.

Treat any result which is at odds with 'common sense' with suspicion

The forecaster must listen to his instinct. A numerate person has an instinctive understanding of and feel for numbers. Thus a forecast which feels wrong probably is wrong. Where the detail of the forecast is rechecked, an error may come to light. In some instances the forecast may have incorporated a new factor or an influence which had previously been overlooked.

It will be a fluke for a forecast to be exactly fulfilled

When the margins of error of most economic and social statistics are taken into account, along with the uncertainties surrounding the future, the odds against a forecast being exactly right are vast. The successful forecaster will be able to reach conclusions which are in the right 'ball park' – close enough to have given a dependable guide.

The forecaster who boasts of making an exact forecast shows signs of immaturity or inexperience, since it will be a fluke to be exactly right. The forecaster must, on average, be more right than wrong. Facing up to the uncertainties means identifying the alternative scenarios and putting the betting odds on each set of forecasts. Even where the customer – the user of the forecasts – requires a single set of figures, some guidance as to the uncertainty and riskiness of the forecast scenario must be given by putting a range around the forecast numbers and the betting odds.

What makes a successful forecaster?

Confronted by all the world's uncertainties, the forecaster must be equipped with a sound judgement. Shrewdness, wisdom and judgement come with age and experience, and it is foolish to expect the young to be capable of balanced judgement in compiling a forecast. A brilliant mathematician may not be capable of compiling a sound set of forecasts without the knowledge of the available data and the judgement to know what to accept or reject. Some people never achieve shrewdness and judgement and most of us will know individuals who have gone through life making a series of mistakes. We do not necessarily learn from our mistakes.

Apart from the indispensable asset of good judgement, the forecaster must be numerate and have a feel for history. A sound knowledge of economic and political history is invaluable, not least because it generates an understanding of human motivation. It also helps cultivate an understanding of change and the pace of change. Without this it is extremely difficult to make dependable estimates of the impact of new technology and the time scale in which changes will take effect.

Some aspects of life are extremely deep rooted. In the USA, for example, the legacy of the Civil War remains deeply entrenched in parts of the south. On one occasion, I was sent to the south to explore the prospects of developing a business connection for the management of investment funds. To my astonishment, I found a deep hostility to New York and a preference for dealing with London.

The religious divisions remain acute and hostility between Muslim and Hindu, Protestant and Catholic are still a major factor in large parts of world society. Some divisions are lessening and old hatreds in Europe, reaching back to the Franco-Prussian war, have been smothered in the formation and development of the Common Market. Nevertheless, an awareness of the political roots of Europe, the USA and all trading nations is a useful tool of the forecaster.

This applies equally in the field of social change. The drive towards equality in the areas of religion, the abolition of slavery, female equality, racial equality and age equality are part of a continuing chain of social change with profound economic consequences. The forecaster must allow for the effects of these changes in his work, recognizing the fall in female fertility and the ageing of the population as measurable trends with powerful implications for future spending and political and economic change.

The forecaster therefore needs a broad body of knowledge to harness to his disciplines as a forecaster. There is a growing tendency for more intense specialization in work and business. This is unlikely to be reversed. Nevertheless, in looking for a dependable forecaster we need to step back in time to the days when an intelligent person had a wide spectrum of knowledge and understanding, such as characterized many of the original members of the Royal Society in the latter part of the 17th century. We need all-rounders, filled with the curiosity to keep abreast of change and with the ability to set change, whether in the political economy or the sciences, into perspective.

BIBLIOGRAPHY

Ashton, David & Simister, Leslie – *The Role of Forecasting in Corporate Planning*; Staples Press, London 1970.

Browning, Iben & Winkless, Nels – *Climate and the Affairs of Men*; Fraser 1975.

Buchanan, R.A. – *The Power of the Machine*; Viking 1992.

Buffet, Warren – 'Letters to Shareholders', – annual reports; Berkshire Hathaway Inc.

Carswell, John – *The South Sea Bubble*; Alan Sutton Publishing 1993.

Climate Impacts Review Group for the Department of the Environment – *Review of the Potential Effects of Climate Change in the United Kingdom*; HMSO March 1996.

Cooper, Robert – *The Post-Modern State and the World Order*; Demos London 1997.

The *Currency Forecaster*, monthly – Informa Publishing.

The Darwin College Lectures – Predicting the Future; Cambridge University Press 1993.

Demographic Yearbook – United Nations.

Ellinger, A.G. – *The Art of Investment*; Bowes & Bowes Publishers 1955.

Fildes, Robert – *World Index of Economic Forecasts*; Gower 1995.

Fisher, P.A. – *Common Stocks and Uncommon Profits*; John Wiley & Sons 1996.

Galbraith, J.K. – *The Great Crash 1929*; Penguin Books 1954 and 1975.

Galbraith, J.K. – *The Culture of Contentment*; Houghton Mifflin US 1992.

Galbraith, J.K. – *A Short History of Financial Euphoria*; Penguin Books 1994.

Graham, Benjamin, Cottle, Sidney & Dodd, David L. – *Security Analysis*; McGraw-Hill 1962.

Ho Mae-Wan – *Genetic Engineering, Dream or Nightmare?*; Gateway 1998.

Huxley, Aldous – *Brave New World*; Chatto & Windus 1932.

Intergovernmental Panel on Climate Change – *The Regional Impact of Climate Change*; Cambridge University Press 1997.

International Financial Statistics; IMF annually.

Jay, Peter – *Road to Riches and the Wealth of Man*; Weidenfeld & Nicolson 2000.

Kennedy, Paul – *Preparing for the Twenty First Century*; Harper Collins 1993.

Keynes, J.M. – *The General Theory of Employment, Interest and Money*; Macmillan 1936.

Khalizad, Zelmay & Lesser, Ian – *Sources of Conflict in the 21st Century*; Rand 1998.

Kindleberger, Charles P. – *Manias, Panics and Crashes: A History of Financial Crises*; John Wiley & Sons 1997.

Landes, David – *The Wealth and Poverty of Nations*; Little, Brown 1998.

Leslie, John – *The End of the World*; Routledge 1996.

Loeb, Gerald M. – *The Battle for Investment Survival*; John Wiley & Sons 1995.

Lowe, Janet – *Value Investing Made Easy: Benjamin Graham's Classic Investment Strategy Explained for Everyone*; McGraw-Hill 1996.

Mackay, Charles – *Extraordinary Popular Delusions and the Madness of Crowds*; John Wiley & Sons, originally published in 1841.

'Main Economic Indicators'; OECD, monthly.

Meadows, D.H., Meadows, D.L. & Randers, J. – *Beyond the Limits*; Post Mills, Chelsea Green 1992.

Meadows, D.H., Meadows D.L., Randers, J. & Behrends, W.H. – *The Limits to Growth*; New York, New American Library 1972.

Milne, Thomas E. – *Business Forecasting: A Managerial Approach*; Longman 1975.

Monitoring the World Economy 1827–1992; OECD 1995.

Mulvaney, J.E. & Mann, C.W. – *Practical Business Models*; William Heinemann 1976.

The OECD Jobs Study: Evidence and Explanations; OECD 1995.

Phelps Brown, E.H. & Hopkins, Sheila V. – 'Seven Centuries of the Prices of Consumables Compared with Builders' Wage Rates'; *Economica* Nov. 1956.

Rifkin, Jeremy – *The End of Work*; G.T, Putman's Sons 1995.

Robinson, Colin – *Business Forecasting: An Economic Approach*; Thomas Nelson, London 1971.

Rolt, L.T.C. – *Victorian Engineering*; Pelican Books 1974.

Rose, H.B. – *The Economic Background to Investment*; Cambridge University Press 1960.

Rostow, W.W. – *The World Economy*; Macmillan 1978.

Silver, Lee – *Remaking Eden*; Weidenfeld & Nicolson 1998.

Soros, George – 'The Capitalist Threat'; *Atlantic Monthly*, January 1997.

Statistical Yearbook; United Nations.

Stekler, Herman O. – *Economic Forecasting*; Longman 1970.

Thorneycroft, Terry – *Seasonal Patterns in Business and Everyday Life*; Gower 1987.

Tylecote, Andrew – *The Long Wave in the World Economy*; Routledge 1991.

Weaver, Denis – *Investment Analysis*; Longman 1971.

Wellings, Fred – *Forecasting Company Profits*; Woodhead Publishing 1998.

Weltman, Jeremy C. – 'Consensus Forecasts'; *A Digest of International Economic Forecasts*, monthly; Consensus Economics Inc.

Wood, Douglas & Fildes, Robert – *Forecasting for Business*; Longman 1976.

World Economic and Social Survey; United Nations, annually.

'The World in Figures'; *The Economist*, annually.

The World Health Report 1995, Bridging the Gaps; World Health Organisation.

World Population Prospects: the 1994 Revision; United Nations.

INDEX